Barbara L. Wegener

Cover Art by Kaitlin and Jeremiah Bauer

WESTBOW
PRESS®
A DIVISION OF THOMAS NELSON
& ZONDERVAN

WestBow Press books may be ordered through booksellers or by contacting:

WestBow Press
A Division of Thomas Nelson & Zondervan
1663 Liberty Drive
Bloomington, IN 47403
www.westbowpress.com
1 (866) 928-1240

Scripture taken from the Holy Bible, NEW INTERNATIONAL VERSION®. Copyright © 1973, 1978, 1984 by Biblica, Inc. All rights reserved worldwide. Used by permission. NEW INTERNATIONAL VERSION® and NIV® are registered trademarks of Biblica, Inc. Use of either trademark for the offering of goods or services requires the prior written consent of Biblica US, Inc.

ISBN: 978-1-5127-4709-6 (sc)
ISBN: 978-1-5127-4711-9 (hc)
ISBN: 978-1-5127-4710-2 (e)

Library of Congress Control Number: 2016910136

Print information available on the last page.

WestBow Press rev. date: 7/7/2016

CHAPTER 1

INTO THE DEPTHS

Cara was nine years old when her mother died. *Well,* she remarked to herself, *I guess that's that.* She couldn't remember a time in her life when her mother wasn't sick, either from the cancer, the treatment, or the infection she got while in the hospital. Exactly what killed her mother didn't matter. Her mother was dead, and that was final. The future had little importance at this point. Time had ended.

During the last year of her mother's illness, Cara had become subdued, stuck in a morbidity about life. She had learned to help her mom through all kinds of unrelenting conditions–way too many of those–and enjoyed the fleeting times when her mom had a reprieve from her sentence. They both knew that heaven was the only hope of relief. Her mom looked forward to it. Cara became reticent, waiting for the end for them both–whatever that meant.

And now it was here. Cara had never looked beyond this moment–didn't know how to, didn't know what to expect. So she accepted it as she had everything else: expect nothing, enjoy the few moments when happiness intervenes, and just wait. To say the least, she was totally unprepared for what did come next: a man, dressed like a pastor, showed up unannounced at the funeral, saying he was her father. Cara's reticence had become her guard, a stubbornness rooted in her understanding about life that would give no quarter to anyone. If this man was to be the next chapter of her life, she would accept it as just that. Who really knew what was to be the future? Her face and actions belied no evidence of approval or disdain.

To add to the surprise, this man came with a woman and several children—a girl, the oldest, and two boys, both younger than she. He introduced them as his "family", a word distant and impervious to her.

"She's too young to understand what's going on," said the woman, and Cara betrayed no reaction to this observation.

The three children stared at her; no one said a word. While Cara's mind was aflutter with queries, she had learned a defensive attitude toward others: you counted on no one, you expected nothing; that way, there would be no disappointment. As her mother would say, "Each day is replete with its own problems; no need to add to it with hopes that will lead to sadness later."

As the funeral progressed, there was one thing the preacher said that spoke to Cara's heart: he talked freely about heaven, and that Cara's mother was now resting in the arms of Jesus. Her mom had used words like that, and Cara found it to be a settling moment, a bit of peace in this confusion. And, there were other words as well, things her mother had read to her from the Bible, words like, "the resurrection from the dead", and "because He lives, we will live also." Cara knew this was about Jesus, and while it gave her spirit some relief, still her demeanor belied no emotion. Would any of this make a difference? Her mother was dead, and that was that.

CHAPTER 2

THE SURPRISE VISITORS

The funeral took place on a typical steamy August afternoon, a Monday, in the town of Live Oak in northern Florida. The gathering at the cemetery went quickly as everyone wanted to get back into the air conditioning. Cara longed to stay by the casket; once it was buried, her mother would truly be gone from her. After the final prayer, she watched as the casket was lowered, then joined the on-lookers as they tossed a flower in a last effort of remembrance, and maybe to bring a spirit of beauty to what had transpired…if that was possible.

The ride to her grandparents' house was filled with a quiet sadness accompanied by an ominous air of uncertainty. Cara had a feeling that something was wrong, beyond her mother's death, something new and unexpected. Her grandparents were arguing, voices low, their words clipped and angry. She decided it had to do with the strange man, the pastor, who had attended the funeral with his family.

"Showing up like this! What right does he have after all these years…" she heard her gramma say.

"She belongs as much to him. He did send money every month to help support them. And remember, Karina spoke freely about forgiveness. We have to respect that." Her grandpa's voice was soft but full of authority. "Let's get through the rest of this afternoon first. No need to add to the troubles right now."

The rest of the ride was quiet, the car filled with a silence that clung to Cara in shrouded mystery. What did her grandpa mean, 'No need to add to the troubles right now?' Was there something that Cara had done, or not done? Her mind was tinkering with this when they arrived, the house already filled with people. Some of them she recognized as people from the church. Others were ladies who had visited her mother over the years; Cara was never part of those visits, being told she could play in the other room.

Cara never played. She took care of her mother. That was her job, her responsibility. Hadn't her grandmother told her that? "You be a good girl and take care of your momma." And she had. Or, at least she thought she had. Now her mother was dead, and life was at a standstill. Maybe she hadn't done everything she should have, and this was the result. Maybe this was the "troubles" grandpa alluded to.

Inside her grandparents' house, Cara decided it was a grown-ups only event since there was no one else her age. She decided it would be best to stay out of the way, to go play in the other room, as it were. She sat respectfully on a chair by a window not far from the front door, pretending she wasn't really there, her aloneness the most salient comment on her life. Furthermore, she thought to herself, being this close to the door would enable her to leave, if she needed to. This was an adult gathering; she probably wouldn't even be missed. In fact, from here she could walk to the apartment she and her mother had shared and called home.

For now, she sat and observed as the visitors chatted together, their plates filled with the traditional foods brought to such an event. Occasionally someone would come over to Cara in an effort to include her in conversation. "Well, Cara," they would say, "your momma is at rest now."

Yes, she was.

"What do you think is going to happen to you?"

What that meant, Cara had no idea. Maybe they thought she would get sick and die the same way.

"I suppose you'll live with your grandparents now."

In Cara's mind, she had her own place to go to. She had taken care of her mom there for years–she could take care of herself there now. And besides, she wasn't sure her grandparents' house was the best place for her. When she and her mom had moved out a little over four years ago, harsh words were spoken, and there were plenty of bad feelings. Cara's name had been a central theme, and she believed she was to blame. Why would they take her in now?

The party was suddenly interrupted with the arrival of the young pastor and his family. The hush that fell over the entire house was quite sudden and distinct. Something unexpected was going on. Cara didn't know them, but obviously her grandfather did. He walked quickly, his steps heavy on the floor, meaning to intercept them at the door; he spoke with a quiet harshness in his voice that sent electrical currents through the room.

"Not now, not here! I told you to wait!"

But the man's wife stepped in front and produced such a stern look that her grandfather noticeably changed; he actually invited the family to come in and get something to eat. He and the pastor, however, went out on the porch, unaware they had taken their places outside the window where Cara was sitting. There were matters that had to be settled, apparently, and Cara could hear her grandpa's deep voice in pointed conversation.

"I'm not sure this is best. You don't know Cara; this really isn't the time to separate her from what she's used to. She's used to us. At least give us time to explain things to her, to let her adjust, somehow…"

"I understand your concern, but I think it best we make the change now. Her life is in turmoil anyway. Why make her go through it again when she does come to live with us? And, she is going to come live with me and my family. You understand that, right?" The pastor's words made no sense to Cara. They weren't really meant for her ears, but the mistake had been made. Who was this man, and why did he think she should go live with him? What right did he have to say this?

Her eyes began looking around at the people inside the house. Several people had engaged the mother in conversation, as if they knew her. Cara wondered, even more now, why they had come, who they were, and what was happening. Still, she sat in the corner, doing her best to be invisible. It wasn't working.

The oldest child had made her way over to Cara. At ten years old, she was only slightly taller, but she seemed to possess an aura that was more confrontational than friendly. Cara looked away.

"You're Cara, aren't you? I'm Katie, and I have to share my room with you." She spoke pointedly, the message delivered as though it was fact, like it was already decided, and Cara had nothing to say about it. Then it hit her. Wait. What was she talking about? What room?

Cara stood up abruptly, facing the girl, her manner equally hostile. "I don't know what you're talking about. I have my own place, my own room."

And with that, Cara searched for her grandmother in an effort to discover the truth about these intruders. As Cara approached her, she became witness to another, equally disturbing conversation.

"Are you and your husband in agreement about this?" Her grandmother's comments caused Cara to stop in her tracks. Again.

"Actually, no, we're not." The mother's voice was almost loud enough for everyone in the house to hear. "On my part, we both have busy jobs that take a lot of time and energy. I'm not sure I have time for one more person to look after; we have three children of our own, and we don't need another child. Well, especially not Cara."

"Then why did you agree to take her?" It was then that both women noticed Cara, standing close enough to overhear what had transpired between them. The mother walked off, not wanting to continue the discussion, and Cara looked dumbfounded at her gramma. She sensed anger, just below the surface, about to erupt. Cara felt the same way. Something was going on, and her grandmother, trying to get control of whatever it was, caused Cara even greater confusion.

Gramma bent down next to Cara, fumbling to explain. "We had planned to have some time to tell you about this, but I'm sorry, that's not going to happen." And she looked away, holding back the tears that were beginning to escape from her eyes.

By then Cara's grandfather was standing next to her, and everyone in the room was staring at them, some in wonderment, others in disbelief. His voice was deeper than usual, his sternness more noticeable than anything else. "Cara, this is your family now. This man is your father, and he, his wife, and his children are taking you to live with them."

All faces in the room were fixed on Cara, and as she returned their stares, they slowly turned away, the verdict having been given, the matter finalized.

So, this was to be the sentence for her failure? Well, that's that, she said to herself for the second time in the same day. What other choice did she have? Whoever these people were, she belonged to them now.

CHAPTER 3

ESTRANGEMENT

The car drove out of town, Cara sitting in the back of the van with her new half-sister. All her earthly belongings had been hastily stuffed into four plastic grocery bags, now stowed under her feet. It probably was best this way. Tears had formed in her grandmother's eyes, and her grandfather's voice was shaky with emotion. There were so many questions with no answers, no time for asking. Whatever the events that her mother's death had put in motion, they were being driven by a run-away locomotive. There was no stopping it. Cara would just have to ride the train until it came to the end.

While her insides were churning with fear, her face and demeanor gave nothing away. Obviously what had happened between her grandparents and her mother years earlier was being settled by getting rid of her, now that her mother was dead – even if no one said it. She knew she had been the source of the problem, which, in her mind, was why her mother had died. From now on, she would keep her feelings to herself and just do what she was told. Her mother had said, "There are some things in life you just have to accept. That way they don't hurt you as much." This must be one of them. Accept it; this would protect her from any more of that hurt she was feeling. At least she hoped so.

Driving out of the small town of Live Oak, Cara observed that the scenery was different than she had ever observed in the past. The streets, the houses, the open spaces—she had never been on this road before. Where were they going? Her life was already shifting from the home she had known to some alien existence she could not begin to envision. It was already late in the day, and the sun was beginning to lower in the sky. Shadows of trees and buildings provided an eerie palate that added to a strange fear festering inside her.

The adults in the front seat said nothing for a long while. When they spoke it was soft, not wanting anyone else in the car to hear what was said. The two little boys in the car seats had already drifted off, making soft snoring noises. Such contentment, Cara thought. If only all of life could be that way. The girl next to her, Katie was her name (Cara wasn't sure) looked straight ahead, seemingly oblivious to Cara's presence, occasionally looking out her side window, but never at her. Cara felt numb. Nothing seemed real; maybe, hopefully, it was all just a dream. No. She knew it wasn't, but what else would explain all....*this!*

The drive went on for several hours before they arrived at their destination. Cara had actually fallen asleep somewhere during the journey, and she was startled when the man gently tried to coax her out of the back bench, maybe carry her inside. She quickly stirred, and the man had to put her down.

"It's okay, Cara. This is your home now."

Cara just stared at him, not knowing what to say. He stood for a minute, then left her, standing half in and half out of the van. As everyone got their things out of the car, Katie picked up Cara's bags and shoved them at her.

"Come on!" she ordered. "You can take your own stuff."

The mother carried the sleeping three-year-old as the four-year-old grabbed his toys and followed after. Cara exited the van as well, but she had no idea where she was or where to go. She stood on the sidewalk watching as everyone made their way to the front door of a house; it was as if her feet were shackled to the pavement, and Cara realized how alone she felt.

What was she doing here? What was going to happen to her? 'This is your home now' the man had said.

"Dear Jesus," Cara silently prayed, "what if I don't want this to be my home? What if, after being here for a few days, *they* don't want me anymore?"

Her stomach felt like it contained a covey of helpless chicks stirring up trouble. Confusion, fear, anger, hurt? Everything, all at the same time.

And then, something amazing happened: it seemed like someone, or something, had touched her, maybe the wind, maybe a feather from a bird, a falling leaf; but she heard her mother's words very clearly: "Don't worry, Cara; God will never leave you or forsake you. He loves you very much."

And with that, an ease washed over her, as if a hand had lovingly brushed her back. Slowly, and with her head up, she walked up to the house and went inside.

CHAPTER 4

INTO THE LIONS' DEN

As casually as possible, Cara looked around at her new environment. She knew she was an outsider; however, what she saw was more than she could take in at the moment. The house was large and seemed very new; it was bigger inside than any Cara had ever seen, and the furnishings displayed a decorator's taste. Wow, she almost said aloud! Who lives like this?

As she stood in the entranceway, she saw there was a room just off to the right. The door was slightly ajar, and as she glanced inside, she saw the silhouettes of two desks; there were also many shelves with lots of books and other stuff. Looks like an office, she decided, but whose? And why would a house have its own office?

Turning to look at the rest of the house, she noticed a stairway, just past the office area. There were eight stairs that went up to a landing, then more after a complete turnaround. Must be a second floor, she thought to herself; probably where the bedrooms are. And she wondered how many there were. In the apartment where she and her mom had lived, there was only one, and they both had shared it, as well as the one bed. Well, that's how it came – furnished, her mom had said.

Cara began to take in the rest of the downstairs – a large living room *and* dining room, and a nice sized room next to the stairway.

The mother came out of a room towards the back of the dining room, and Cara watched as a swinging door closed off her view; she decided it was a large kitchen.

"Cara, it's late," the mother said. "You need to go upstairs, to bed. Take your...*bags*.... I'll show you the room Katie is sharing with you." The mother's voice was without emotion, and there was no indication of either kindness or concern as she gave Cara the information.

With the downstairs lights all turned off, and with limited light for the way, Cara almost stumbled as she followed. Well, there was just so much to look at! The mom disappeared on the stairway, and Cara hurried her steps; she arrived at the upper landing in time to be told which room was Katie's.

"Is there a bathroom I could use?" Cara's voice was tentative.

"Katie will show you. Just go to bed now. It's late." And the mother went silently down the hall to a room at the far end.

Inside the bedroom, Katie had already changed clothes, obviously dismayed that she had to be responsible for this sister she wanted no part of.

"Where's the bathroom?" Cara asked flatly.

Katie gruffly took Cara's arm and shoved her towards the door, opened it, and pointed to a room across the hall. "And be quiet when you come back. Everyone else is probably asleep already."

"What am I supposed to do with my stuff?" Cara's inquiry brought an angry glare.

"I don't really care. This is *my* room." Then, thinking it over, Katie tauntingly added, "Just put your bags on the *floor* over by your side of the bed. Yeah. That'll be your space. Just keep your junk out of my way! It probably has cooties!"

Cara decided not to respond. It was late, the day had been long and filled with too much drama as it was; if this was to be her home, she'd have to make the best of it.

Obviously, no one else here neither cared for nor wanted her. Maybe, by the end of the week, they'd all come to the same understanding and take her back home. With that, she took care of her needs; then as quietly as possible, she made her way back and into bed. Proud of herself for not getting lost, or disturbing anyone, she actually smiled, briefly, and laid down.

But now her mind began to wonder back over the day's events. Her mother's funeral seemed so very long ago – was she really dead and buried? At this thought, everything began to blur. Had her grandparents really allowed these people to take her? Why? Afraid of the answer, she tried to erase it all and just fall asleep. Eventually, exhaustion took over, her eyelids became heavy, and, remembering the message she had heard just before entering this house, she simply fell asleep.

CHAPTER 5

THE NEW FAMILY

It was Tuesday, Cara's first full day in this surreal existence. She decided to just blend in, her intent to be unnoticed. She needed to learn the household routine and do the jobs she was assigned, things like helping to clear the table, sweeping the kitchen floor, and taking charge of her own property in the bedroom Katie had to share with her. Easy, she thought to herself. No one seemed to be aware that her life over the past several years meant taking care of her mother through her illnesses, being the main caretaker in the small apartment that had been their home. Neither did anyone seem to sense the sorrow Cara kept hidden inside; nor would Cara allow it to be seen. Weakness at this juncture would not be tolerated, especially not in Cara's mind.

One thing she learned quickly was that this family did everything by a schedule. You were expected to be dressed and at breakfast at 8:00 AM. After that, chores were to be done before anything else, and then you were expected to busy yourself with appropriate, useful activities.

On this day, the dad left for work as soon as he had finished breakfast. Cara had no idea what he did, but he seemed to be in a hurry. Then Katie left the house, with the mother's permission of course, and the two little boys followed their mother around. She quickly grew weary of them and put them in the family room just off the kitchen. Cara wasn't sure if she was allowed in there, never having been given a tour of the living spaces. Sitting alone at the kitchen table she had difficulty figuring out what to do with herself. Apparently, she was invisible since no one took any notice of her presence.

Tears began forming in her eyes, and she gave herself a mental scolding; she had no intention of showing weakness. This was her life, now. Be strong! Don't bring any shame on yourself!

Remembering the bookshelf in Katie's bedroom, she went upstairs and found a book she hadn't yet read. She brought it downstairs, and, sitting comfortably on a couch in the living room, opened the book and began to peruse the chapters. It didn't take long for her to become completely immersed in the story and unaware of her surroundings. What a surprise when two pairs of eyes suddenly appeared over the top of her book! Two little boys began to giggle their delight at her reaction to their mischief.

"So!" Cara said. "You must be Jacob, and you're 4 years old; and you must be Samuel, and you're 3. Am I right?"

The boys shook their heads in turn. "You're Cara!" they responded. "And you're our new sister! Wanna play with us?"

This put a whole new perspective on the family. A smile began inside Cara that hadn't been there in days. "Okay. Now that we're acquainted, what shall we play?"

Each boy took one of Cara's hands and led her to the large room next to the stairway. It was their playroom, they told her, and she was amazed by the size of the room; the three large plastic bins on the floor must have contained every toy imaginable. The shelves as well were crowded with action figures, trucks, airplanes, and stuffed animals, enough to open a toy store. Everywhere she looked held the promise of unimaginable fun that would easily fill the rest of the morning...and then some!

Cara sat down in the middle of the floor, waiting for the boys to choose their fantasy and wondering what she should do. But the boys' imaginations were well under way as each one chose a truck and began making truck noises. They drove their vehicles around the room and around Cara; then they drove on her and over her while she pretended to be a monster trying to catch them and gobble them up, occasionally grabbing one and tickling him until he was joined by the other for some of the same treatment. Suddenly, a noise was heard – the creaking of someone coming down the stairs – and the ruckus came to an abrupt stop! The two boys began to play nice with each other, and with Cara, which was the comment made by the mother as she glanced into the room on her way past it.

While that was the end of the loud playing, the three spent the next hour building roads that wound around the room, picking up or delivering imaginary items. Cara sometimes watched, but other times inserted questions to clarify the story. As the morning came to a close, Cara began to feel more at ease, almost as if she could actually stay here, if she had to.

The next meal was promptly at 12:00 noon. Although it wasn't her job, Cara made herself available to help. No, the mother said at first, then changed her mind and let Cara set out the dishes that were appropriate for the meal. Katie arrived in time to get drinks ready, which was one of her chores. The dad showed up several minutes late, and he quickly took his place at the head of the table, apologizing for making everyone wait. He announced that he had arranged to have the afternoon at home; there was a planning committee meeting at church that evening – something about finalizing the plans for a new fall worship schedule. While Cara wondered what that meant, she was thankful that the dad was involved with a church. That meant they would be attending Sunday services. Good. Otherwise she'd really have problems. She and her mom and grandparents *always* went to church; well, her mom had missed a lot when she was sick.

With that thought, Cara's eyes began to water, memories of her mother bringing back a sadness she had tried to keep in check. Quickly, she lowered her face, hoping no one witnessed her weakness. If they had, she would say she had something in her eye. But no one said a word. Cara ate her sandwich, choking down each bite. She would excuse herself, if this problem continued. The family, however, all seemed to be in their own worlds. If she had looked up, Cara would have noticed that no one was looking at anyone. Except the two little boys. They were making faces at each other, which brought the mother's attention as they giggled instead of ate. With a glare, that stopped quickly.

"Since you're home this afternoon, I'm going to run up to my classroom to pick up a few things I need to work on before next week." From the look on the dad's face, the mother's announcement was not what he wanted to hear. She continued, "I'll take Katie along, so Dan, you're in charge of the two boys." The mother had spoken, and the matter was decided.

The dad thought otherwise. "Why don't you take Cara along, too? That way she can…"

But the dad never had a chance to finish his statement. Both the mother and Katie were very vocal concerning that idea. "No, dear," the mother stated adamantly. "She's *your* responsibility. Not mine. Not Katie's. That's what we decided, remember?"

"No, that's not what we decided! We're family! All of us! That's what we said." Cara was dumbfounded! What were they talking about? Why was the dad so angry?

And why did they talk about her as if she wasn't there? It didn't matter to her if she didn't go along with the mom and Katie. But what was this about "family"? She wasn't part of this family, so why was the dad so upset?

The mother had the last word. "You can say what you want. Katie and I are going up to the school. We are not taking Cara. What you do with her is your business." Before the dad could respond, the two of them cleared their plates and left – they were out the door, in the van, and down the street just that quickly.

Dan sat for a while, still angry, not knowing what to say or how to approach Cara.

She was quick to notice his discomfort. "I can clean up the lunch stuff, if you have other things to do. I don't mind." While there were many questions floating around in Cara's head, that's what came out first.

Dan breathed a big sigh and moved his head back and forth, like he was saying, "No," which Cara thought he was, meaning that she was wrong, or something!

Finally, the dad spoke. "No, Cara, I'll take care of this. You probably don't know where everything goes, and Maggie is very particular about her kitchen." He cleaned up the two boys and took them to their playroom. After getting them settled with some toys, he returned to the kitchen. By then, Cara had already put the dirty dishes in the dishwasher and was beginning to put the leftovers away.

"I know what I'm doing," she said softly. "I helped my mom and my grandma a lot at home, and I saw where everything came from when I helped get the lunch on."

This caught the dad off guard. "Okay. Well, good," he managed to say. And instead of using the opportunity to talk with Cara, to try to explain things, Dan chose to avoid the situation. Instead, he went into the office and closed the door.

Unknowingly, Cara was witnessing the dysfunction in this family; she had become the target of their unspoken problems. Had she known this outwardly, she would have spoken up, or at least been more proactive on her own behalf. Her sweetness and her naiveté were her salvation and her downfall, and this kept her from getting on the phone to tell her grandparents to come and get her. But would they? She simply believed that this was to be her home now. That's what she had been told, and there was nothing she could do about it.

The afternoon went slowly. After finishing in the kitchen, she mainly sat back down in the living room and read the book she had found. Once she got up and checked on the two boys, but they were sleeping, deep into naps. Sometime later, the dad came out of the office, but he said very little to her and just went upstairs.

Deciding she had the downstairs to herself, she began snooping around, still curious about everything. Her first steps took her to the family room she had noticed when they ate lunch, just off the kitchen. It wasn't as well kept as the living/dining room, and the furniture looked much more comfortable – used, she told herself. Here was the television as well. The downstairs bathroom was adjacent to the room, and there was a door on the other side of it that opened into the playroom. She headed back into the kitchen, curious to see what could be in all those cupboards, but a noise outside scared her; she flew back to the couch in the living room and put her nose in her book. She did not want to get caught doing something suspicious.

The noise turned out to be nothing, but Cara decided to stay put. She was comfortable – well, sort of – and she had something to occupy her mind. At least it was a diversion from the reality of her situation. Once again her mind drifted back to her former home. Had she thought it a possibility, she would have gone to the phone and called her grandparents. Certainly they didn't know what this family was like, or they never would have allowed them to take her.

But maybe they did know. Maybe she was the only one who was clueless about all this. What would her mother think if she knew…. Cara's mind came to a sudden stop, reality striking again. Tears began welling in her eyes, running down her cheeks. Quickly she rubbed them away. This behavior was unacceptable, she told herself. She should never show her vulnerability in this house! These people were strangers. Who knows what would happen to her if she let down her guard!

Putting her own thoughts aside, she once more tried to focus on reading the book. Every so often her mind would begin to wander back to her strange circumstances; and just as quickly, she would mentally discipline herself to avoid thinking of her mother's death and her new life. Without realizing it, a tiredness began to take over, and Cara laid her head down on the couch. In a very short time, she fell asleep.

It was hours before the mom and Katie returned. Their arrival woke Cara, and she tried to avoid looking sleepy. But they never even seemed to notice her. The dad emerged from somewhere in the house, and his questions as to their whereabouts received an on-going list of information. Besides going to the school, the mother said, they had run some errands, including bringing supper from a fast food chicken place. That way they could get the evening meal out of the way, and the dad could make his meeting at church.

No one said a word to Cara, and she wasn't sure if she should help in the kitchen or not. Since Katie was in there with the mom, Cara just sat silently on the couch in the living room. Once more she pretended to be reading; but she was more interested in what else was going on. Even the two little boys had left their playroom and gone into the kitchen. She heard talking, but none of it loud enough for her to decipher. The dad had gone upstairs, and she thought about just going into the family room, almost like she belonged here. But she just stayed put, unsure of her position in this group of people.

Soon, the dad invited Cara into the kitchen where supper was served. Talk around the table concerned what the mother and Katie had done all day, the places they went, and what had been done at school. None of it made much sense to Cara, but she sat politely and pretended to listen. Since no one inquired about her day, she didn't have pretend about anything; she was safe, for now. Even her brief escapade in touring the house stayed her secret. But Jacob and Samuel eyed her as if they were aware of her investigations …or, maybe they were just being the precious little imps that kept this family together. Whatever it was, Cara smiled back at them which made them giggle.

"Boys! We behave properly at the table. If you're finished eating, excuse yourselves. You can go play in the family room until it's time for bed."

Why was it that when the mother spoke, she sounded more angry than loving? She was obviously the commander of the house, and she dictated orders that everyone obeyed. Just where Cara fit into the house was not yet determined, but Cara was discovering the necessity of staying under the radar.

The dad finished eating and left for his meeting. Cara offered to help clean up the supper, but she was met with silent stares from both the mother and her daughter. "That's not necessary," the mother finally said, and she and Katie continued talking as if she wasn't there.

Cara left the room and returned to the couch in the living room. Maybe it would just take more time for them to get to know her, she decided. Either that, or she would just have to find someplace else to go.

What a puzzle! This family wasn't like any she had ever known. Maybe she had been captured by aliens! That had to be it! When she fell asleep in the car after leaving her grandparents, they took her to their spaceship, and now they were on a whole different planet in a whole different universe! What else would explain their unusual behavior, and the way they treated her? They sure weren't like the people back home in Live Oak! Her mom and her grandparents would never believe…. And then she stopped herself, reality taking its place, again, the hard truth that this was all real. It was her life, now. And she opened the book, looking at the words, trying to get her mind under control. If there was any escape, it would be in reading the book in front of her, and only then, in her mind.

By the time the day ended, Cara had finished the book and returned it to its place on Katie's bedroom shelf. She had the feeling that Katie would not want her to mess with any of her stuff.

It was still early in the evening, but Cara cleaned herself up and went to bed, mainly hoping to avoid Katie and any of the anger she harbored. As little as she knew about her, Cara was sure there were undercurrents full of nastiness, and it would be best to avoid any chance of a private confrontation.

CHAPTER 6

NEW DAY, NEW PROBLEMS

On Wednesday, Cara decided she needed to venture outside herself more. It was after breakfast, the table had been cleared and things put away; the father had left for work. The mother had gone upstairs to make the bed, and Katie had followed. Cara could hear soft undercurrents of an angry discussion between them. Best let that one go, she thought, and decided to check on the two boys. At first they seemed to ignore her. But then Jacob brought her a toy and asked if she wanted to play with it.

Cara joined them on the floor; very quickly she and the boys were playing and laughing and having a good time. They invented a game where they used the toys to build imaginary buildings to smash and then rebuild! The three of them were totally immersed in the fun! They never heard anyone approaching, and just that quickly, the bottom dropped out.

Katie was the first one on the scene. "Stop that! What are you doing! We don't play like that in this house! You know better!" she pointedly exclaimed, grabbing Jacob by the arm. Jacob's eyes got big, and his brother Sammy began to cry.

Soon the mother was in the doorway, her response equal to Katie's outcry: "What's going on here?! What happened?" She picked up the youngest, trying to calm him, but as she looked around at the mess, toys scattered throughout and the room completely disheveled, her anger quickly rose to the top.

As stunned as Cara was, she was unprepared for what came next. "Cara!" the mother said, "Are you responsible for this? You need to clean this up! This family has rules, and you're not here to change them! Look at this mess!" Cara felt as though she was being slapped in the face. "On second thought, no! Just go to your room. You probably have no idea about manners and good behavior and keeping a house clean, living with someone as dysfunctional as your mother must have been!"

Silently, Cara marched up the stairs. What did the mother mean, especially about her own mom? And what had she done? They were just playing, she and the boys, having a fun time! At least that's what she called it. Didn't kids laugh and giggle and make a mess when they played? Apparently not in this house. Mentally she started a list: Stuff that doesn't make sense! Actually, by now, the list was quite long when she thought about it: nobody really talks to each other; there's a feeling that nobody really *likes* each other; nobody seems to really want her here.

Her emotions were raw from all she had been through, and everything created a challenge. What was that comment, that she had no idea about keeping a house clean? What had she done all the time her mother was sick? Didn't anyone here understand what her days had been like? How she was the one responsible for taking care of her mother? And now this. What was to become of her in this house? She found herself fighting back the tears, again, an alone-ness filling her from head-to-toe. Nothing felt right. Who were these people? Why was she here? Would her grandparents even care what she was going through?

Cara stayed upstairs for an hour, lying on the bed, mainly staring at the ceiling and trying to keep her tears in check; then she got up and descended partway down the stairs to check the climate of the house. She heard the mother and Katie talking in the family room; the two little boys must have been with them. That certainly was not the place for Cara. "Now what am I supposed to do," Cara mumbled, almost aloud. Quietly, she tip-toed back upstairs and just sat on the top step. All she wanted to do was become invisible. Since that wasn't possible, she decided she just had to keep out of everyone's way.

Before long boredom took over – she needed some kind of activity. Then it came to her that she could explore the upstairs; well, everyone else was downstairs, and she had the upstairs all to herself. Plus, she was curious: she had never been in a house like this, and she wondered how each room looked. She began by peering into the room where the little boys slept. They each had their own bed, and the sheets and covers were bright and colorful. The walls had large drawings of cartoon characters from *Winnie, the Pooh,* and Cara smiled as she identified each one in her mind. Even the rug on the floor had pathways marked that took each boy to his bed. In the corner was a bookshelf filled with stuffed animals, big books, and more toys. What a great room, Cara thought to herself. "I'd never want to leave it!"

But she did – there were other rooms to go snooping into, and she tiptoed down the hallway to the mother's and father's room. The door was only slightly ajar, and she carefully pushed it open for a better look. Carefully going in, she discovered an enormous room. It was as big as the apartment she and her mom had shared! Even the bathroom was gigantic! The colors, the tile, everything was beautiful in Cara's eyes. She had seen displays like this at her grandpa's store, but she had never imagined a house where people actually lived this way!

Suddenly, there was noise on the stairs. Katie and her mother and the two boys were approaching! Quickly, Cara ran into the hallway and was able to dash into a closet before she was spotted.

The family was talking in hushed voices, almost as if someone would hear them; but they went on by and into another room at the end of the hallway, one Cara hadn't noticed; she took the opportunity to sneak back downstairs before she was caught. She would finish her upstairs sight-seeing some other time.

Well, that was fun – kind of. But what to do now? She hadn't really finished checking out the house, so she began by going into the kitchen and attached family room. She already had some idea what was there, but there were two doors in the kitchen that interested her. One, she found, led to the backyard. While it was inviting, she decided to save that for later. The other door led to the garage, another huge space that she decided was more interesting than the house itself: things were not as well organized here. In one corner were the washer and dryer; an array of garden tools was lined up along the back wall; and there was another door, probably to the back yard. The wall that ran to her left was filled with a menagerie of boxes of various sizes, some with writing on them, others just plain, and all of them pretty much stacked in no particular manner. Cara wondered what they all contained. Well, that would also be reserved for other times of exploring. Right now she was mainly interested in the big picture.

Going back into the house, she checked the location of the other residents and decided it was safe to look around the office. This was a good time to do it since the door was closed but unlocked; it must be okay to go in.

The two desks she had seen before in silhouette were very clear now, sitting side-by-side; while one had a computer with a tower, the other had a lap top. Having learned how to use both of these at her school, she was tempted to try to turn one of them on. Better not, she decided; some other time. Instead, her attention was drawn to the items on the shelves. Besides books, there were folders of different colors, obviously placed in some particular order. This interested her, and she became entranced in this collection, unaware that the mother and Katie had come downstairs. The door to the office was open, which it shouldn't have been, and within seconds Cara was again on the receiving end of a reprimand.

"What are you doing in here? No one goes into this office, do you understand! No one!" Cara scooted out as fast as she could. But where to go now? As she rushed into the living room, the mother and Katie followed. Seems the scolding wasn't finished. "That's the second time today you've caused disruption in this home! What do you have to say for yourself? Well?"

Cara looked straight at the woman. She had nothing to say for herself, except things she shouldn't say to an adult. "I'm sorry," finally came out which seemed to calm the storm.

"Well, at least you have some manners. Why don't you go outside and play or something? Apparently you don't know how to behave inside a house!"

Cara took the cue and scooted out the front door. She sat down on the front porch. It was hot, but this was Florida, and she could put up with the heat. Now, however, what to do? A few minutes passed as she sat and moped, tears escaping down her cheeks. She knew, however, after long months of watching her mother die, that crying only made a person's misery worse. Find something else to do, she told herself; stop dwelling on your problems.

Looking around, she decided to check out the rest of the property. She got up and strode down the front walkway, remembering her approach the first night. Turning to look at the house, she saw that the porch was wide here; but there were no chairs or rockers – not like at her grandparents' where porch sitting was an art. Once again these thoughts reminded her of her sad plight, and she forced herself to again change her perception.

She began to look at the neighborhood. The house where she now was to live sat on the corner of the block. All the houses in the area pretty much looked the same except for some of the colors. This interested Cara for a while, and she observed that the variety gave some character to each domicile.

However, this activity didn't last very long. She needed something to do. Then she noticed the flower beds, if that's what you could call them. More like weed beds she thought, and smiled at her own humor. "I know. I can pull out the weeds," she silently mused. This seemed like a perfectly good way to use her time. It was industrious, helpful, and it gave her something to do. Since it would take a while, she would be out of everyone's way. An extra bonus!

Beginning at the edge of the sidewalk that led into the house, she meticulously cleared out the unwanted foliage section by section. It was late in the morning when she had begun her chore, almost noon in fact, but she worked quickly and was almost to the corner of the house when the dad came home for lunch. At first he didn't notice Cara, just the piles of weeds that had been uprooted. He was almost inside when he did a double take. "Cara? Is that you?"

"Hi." Would he be mad at her too?

"What are you doing? Pulling weeds? That's a never ending job around here. Let me get a trash bag." And he went inside the house.

When he returned, there was no bag. "Mom says lunch is ready. We better go in and eat. We can clean this up later. Better get yourself cleaned up, though."

Did he say "we"? Cara's heart lightened.

She went inside and made sure she had cleaned the dirt off her hands and fingernails before joining the family; they were already eating. No one said a word to her. That was okay. She wasn't really part of this family, she reminded herself.

After lunch, the dad kept his promise and spent a good hour helping Cara clean up the mess. Although she had many questions about who he was and why she had been brought to this house to live, she wasn't sure how to pose them. They were working together, but there was this strange distance, an awkwardness, and Cara could find no words that would build a bridge to the answers she needed.

But then he left, had to get back to work he said, and she was once more alone; her mind began wondering into an emptiness where only sadness reigned. "NO!" she almost shouted out loud! And she forced herself to continue getting rid of the weeds that had taken root around the entrance to this house.

She spent the rest of the afternoon outside, finishing the work to clean up the areas on both sides of the steps and across the front of the house. Wandering further, she checked around the sides. Should she continue trying to pull out all the weeds? Maybe. As hot as she was, going inside was not a good alternative, so she convinced herself to just take a break. She went back to the front porch and sat down, fairly weary, trying to keep her mind off her problems.

Eventually the dad returned for supper. By then, Cara was more than ready to go inside. She was hot and thirsty, and her stomach was empty.

"Well, you finally decided to come in the house," the mother commented. "What were you doing out there all day?" Her manner of speaking sounded critical.

What should she say? 'Oh, your front area was full of weeds, so I cleaned it all up for you.' Or, 'I sat on the porch, since I didn't want to come inside and be criticized.' Instead, Cara said nothing; it was supper, time to eat, and everyone sat around the table like there was nothing new in the universe to discuss. Cara herself sat quietly, not wanting to cause discord.

Two days with this family, and Cara's sense of being alone intensified. She was an orphan. Whoever these people were, their lives and their lifestyle were nothing she understood, foreigners to Cara's former life. And the crueler questions again surfaced: Why had her grandparents let them take her away? If she called them, would they even come to get her? Was this man really her *father*? What did that mean? Who were these people? A list of questions flooded her consciousness; unfortunately, she could conceive of no answers.

But there was another thought, even more disparaging, that came into her mind: she wondered if they even *knew God*! To Cara, this was strange. In her former life, God's presence permeated each day: there was Bible reading, talking about God, and many prayers. He was part of everything that went on. But in this house, other than a cross on the wall and a comment about a meeting at church, there was nothing to prove they even recognized that there was a God. They never seemed to pray, like before meals and at bedtime, and in two days, she never heard or saw them read from the Bible. Something wasn't right in this family.

The evening finally came, and the second day with this family showed signs of ending. The dad was in the office, finishing some work on the computer. The mother and Katie had gone upstairs, getting the two boys ready for bed; Cara heard her step-sister making angry overtones to the mother before going to her own room. Cara sat alone in the living room, not wanting to go upstairs and get caught up in Katie's anger.

"Oh, Lord," she mumbled to herself, "what's going to happen to me? Why did you bring me here? Are you even in this house? I feel so alone." Then, as if someone had opened a window, a burst of fresh air surrounded Cara, lingering and caressing, soothing her spirit. Was this God? Was He talking to her? As she waited, she felt a calmness wash away her anxiety; shortly, she made her way up the stairs, now ready for the day to end.

That night before she climbed into bed, and for the first time since she had been brought to this house, she knelt on the floor and softly spoke the prayer her mother had taught her years ago. Soon after she had laid down, she heard Katie mumble something indistinguishable. But Cara paid her no heed. For the first time since her arrival, she fell asleep in a semblance of peace.

CHAPTER 7

A VERY UNEXPECTED SURPRISE

The next day, Thursday, was a definite improvement. The father stayed home, so everyone slept in a little bit later. They had a bigger breakfast, and everyone pitched in to clean it up. They even washed the dishes by hand and put them away.

"What shall we do today?" the father asked. "Summer break will be over in a little more than a week, and then school starts. I think we should go somewhere, have some fun! What do you think?"

Katie was the first to jump on this and promote an idea. "We can go to the park and go swimming and have a picnic. There's even time for me to call Maribelle and see if she can come along."

Then mother chimed in with her thoughts. "How about that new mall that opened in May. They actually have an in-door ice-skating rink. Sounds like fun to me. I could even get some before-school-shopping done while you watch the kids." She said this with a slight glare at the dad.

"Well, I have another idea," said the father. "We have never been to the theme park in Tampa. What's it called?"

Katie's eyes got big! "You mean Busch Gardens? Can we really go there? Ohhh! I'm calling Maribelle, okay? This will be so much fun!"

The mother was quick to speak. "Wait a minute. I'm not sure I'm ready to corral two little boys around there and call that *fun*. I'm in favor of doing something closer where we can come home if things don't work out." With that, the mother gave a look at Cara as if she might be a problem.

Picking up the hint, Cara said, "That's okay. I don't have to go. I'll stay here. I can even take care of the two boys, if you want me to."

That brought a humorous reaction from everyone. Cara's face blushed in embarrassment, not understanding what she had said that made them all laugh. She looked down, once again feeling like the outsider she knew she was. Finally, the father spoke up. "No, Cara. You're coming along. This is a family event. We can handle the two little guys. They'll have fun! We'll all have fun! And Katie, no Maribelle. Like I said, this is *family*. Mom? Shall we go?"

The agreement made, everyone began preparations for a fun day in Tampa. Having no idea what that meant, Cara went upstairs and sat on the bed, hoping Katie would provide some hints. When she finally came upstairs, it was evident that Katie had been crying. "Can I help?" Cara asked.

"You? No! You're the problem! I wish you had never come here! I could have brought my friend if it wasn't for you!" And with that, she stormed out. Cara followed her downstairs, more unsure of what to do than before. As far as Cara was concerned, Maribelle could come along and she could stay home. So what if she'd miss a trip to Busch Gardens. She didn't even know what that was and why they'd want to go there. And why was Katie so mean to her? She had no idea. Maybe she could ask the dad, if she could ever get him to talk to her. Maybe today.

The preparations were finalized, and everyone got in the car. Sitting next to Katie in the back seat, Cara decided she just didn't understand her, and that it might be better to just leave it alone.

However, she was starting to recognize the tantrums this sister would exhibit inexplicably.

A plan began to formulate in Cara's mind as to how to avoid being the recipient of such anger in the future: she would just run away. In the very back of the van, Cara watched the scenery, trying to pay attention to the streets and houses they were passing. Who knows, she thought; I might need an escape route sometime. But it was all too much, too strange. Where were they? None of the names of places were familiar. They were too far from anything she recognized; mainly, she felt lost. The stores, the businesses, the streets – she had never been in a place so filled with cars, trucks, and buildings like this.

When they finally arrived at the theme park, Cara was beyond amazement at the number of people and sights. She almost lost the family, her senses taken captive by the immensity of things she was seeing, already over-stimulated. Suddenly, the dad took her hand. Cara jumped and almost yanked it away, noticing at the last second who it was. This surprised her. Was she in trouble? Had she done something wrong?

"Come on, Cara! Stay with the family! We don't want to lose you," he said, almost as if he cared. And, he was smiling at her!

"I've never seen anything like this! What are we doing here?" Cara managed to reply.

"We're going to have a good time! That's what we're doing here," her dad said. "Let's stay together, though."

The theme park turned out to be more fun than Cara had ever imagined. The family went to everything together, laughing on some scary rides and eating junk food when they got hungry, browsing through a few shops where even the merchandize was unusual. Later in the day, Cara and the dad watched the two little boys on some kiddy rides as the mother and Katie went off together for some mother/daughter time, as they called it.

Waiting for their return, Cara and the dad sat in the shade, watching the two boys enjoying themselves. The dad sighed a few times as if he wanted to say something. But nothing came out. Cara just didn't get him. He seemed nice, but something was obviously bothering him. He had said he was her father. She had no idea why he said that, or what that meant. And for whatever reason, he was unable, or unwilling, to explain it to her. She decided it maybe had something to do with Katie's outburst earlier in the day – 'You're the problem!' Inside, Cara was sure she'd find out somehow.

It was almost an hour before Katie and her mom returned. They had purchased "Mother/Daughter" t-shirts, each showing them off to the family, Katie making sure Cara noticed. Cara, on the other hand, acted as though she didn't care. "She isn't my mother," she thought, and Katie wasn't her friend, so why should it matter to her? Still, something inside tugged at her emotions – she yearned for a life that was now past, for the mother she no longer had – and it was all she could do to stifle some rebellious tears that began seeping from her eyes.

She glanced to the side, cautiously wiping her face, and focused on obscure objects in the distance; she was not aware that the father was a witness to her reaction. Still, he said nothing, did nothing.

As the day was wearing down, the tired family made their way to the exit, feet dragging, minds numbed by the day's events. It took a while to find the van, and when they did, everyone slowly took his or her place, settling in for the long journey home.

Very little was said as they traveled, and the dad noticed everyone's heads seemed to bob to the motion of the van. Well, he thought to himself, tummies had been filled with sweets, eyes with wonder, and minds on overload with excitement. Certainly, this had been a good day! Except for one thing: when he had the chance, why hadn't he been able to find the words to tell Cara who she was and why he had brought her to live with this family? Maybe he didn't know why. Maybe he should have thought it all through before he took the initiative to upend her life. Maybe this was more about him, dealing with his past, than about taking care of this daughter. "Lord," he silently prayed, "What do I do? Show me, and I will do it."

By the time they got home, it was late and everyone was exhausted. Dan parked the van and helped get the two sleeping boys extracted from their seats. Katie followed her mom into the house, and Cara slowly stumbled up the stairs to the door, her body still more asleep than not. As she went inside, she admitted to herself that maybe things wouldn't be as bad with this family as she had expected. She went upstairs and got ready for bed. Unfortunately, the day wasn't over, and Cara was innocently unaware of what was about to take place at the hands of her step-sister.

CHAPTER 8

THE TRUTH

The day at the theme park was just about the most fun Cara had ever had. Now home, all she wanted to do was retire for the day. Exhausted, she fell into bed and was almost asleep when Katie came into the room. Standing at the end of the bed, Katie clenched her teeth, and her hushed onslaught began. "I don't see why you have to live here! This is *my* house! *My* family! *My* room! Now I have to put up with *you!* I couldn't even bring Maribelle along today because of you! Can't you see you're not wanted here? Why don't you just *go away!*"

Cara was dumbfounded! Where had this come from? Hadn't they had a great day? She thought so. Did she miss something? She had been close to falling asleep, but now her mind began to spin. What had she done? Questions berated her brain, but she said nothing. What possible response could there be? Katie was right, the people in this family seemed to just tolerate her presence. And the man who said he was her "father"? Even he didn't know what to do with her.

Just go away, Katie had said, but where would she go? The trip today proved that she didn't know where she was, so how could she go someplace else? She seriously considered just hiding somewhere, like in the garage. Maybe she could live out there, sneak inside to get some food, and just keep out of everyone's way...except for all the bugs and heat and stuff...maybe there was even a boogie-man! No, that wouldn't work.

Maybe she could run away, if it came to that, but where to? All she was sure of was that she was a long way from home...well, from the place where she grew up, anyway. She had no home. That was the problem. Would anyone take her in? No, even her grandparents had just let these strangers abduct her. And for all she knew, Live Oak, where they lived, was in another country. She should have paid better attention to the route when she was first brought here. But, she hadn't. She had fallen asleep! Why had she been so careless?!

Her eyes threatened to tear, but she would not let Katie see that. Best to maintain a hard outer shell and not let anything in that might hurt. Hadn't she learned that while taking care of her mom? *Expect nothing, enjoy the few moments when happiness shows up, then just wait for whatever came next.* Only her mom wasn't here anymore, and it didn't seem like there would be any happiness in her life that was worth waiting for. Not ever! Oh, today was fun. But you couldn't count on building a life of happiness from one day at a theme park.

Shortly, Katie climbed into bed, and Cara slipped under the cover as well, oppressive silence filling every corner of the room. Cara felt hot tears welling up in her eyes, then streaming down her cheeks. She couldn't control them. Afraid that her sobs would alert Katie to this show of weakness, Cara buried her face in her pillow, waiting for the episode to end. She tried to pray, but even that desire was flooded by her emotions. Eventually, the tiredness took over, and she fell asleep. Maybe tomorrow....tomorrow, what? Unknown to Cara, the assault was not over. That had just been round one. Round two would come the next night.

CHAPTER NINE

GOD DOESN'T MAKE MISTAKES

It was Friday, and everyone was worn out from all their fun at Busch Gardens. After a restless night, Cara awoke rather late, and Katie had already dressed and left the house. Katie got to spend the day with her friend, the one she wanted to invite to their theme park adventure but hadn't been allowed to because of Cara. It was the reason for her outburst the night before. All Cara knew was that she would be free of Katie's drama for now.

The day went fairly smoothly overall, since everyone was pretty much in the same boat – still feeling bushed from yesterday's activities at the park. Naps were taken in the afternoon by everyone except the dad. He had to work, so he wasn't present, as usual.

Katie was back at the house by mid-afternoon. And while the day had gone pretty smoothly so far, Cara could tell Katie was constructing the next onslaught in her mind. It was the way Katie's eyes seemed to be glaring at her whenever Cara glanced her way; there were the incidental bumps Cara received whenever Katie passed her; and there were the secret whispers with her mother, after which they both would look at Cara and snicker.

By supper, the dad was home, but the conversation at the table showed the tiring effects of the previous day on him as well. Very little was said until he made a comment on something they had done at the theme park. Then, Jacob and Samuel tried to outdo each other describing a particular ride they had taken; Mom reminded everyone of some silly occurrence; then, Katie brought up the really great presents she and her mom bought, meaning the t-shirts. The ambiance was light-hearted and enjoyable. The only one sitting in silence was Cara. While she had listened to the barrage of laughter, her face retained the detached expression that had saved her over the years. Both parents witnessed her behavior, neither saying a word, attributing the behavior to the previous day's tiring adventures. And, they each mentally noted, she wasn't a real part of the family yet. That would take time, whether Cara wanted to be there or not, and whether the family wanted her…or not.

The rest of the evening repeated the usual pattern of the household. After the dishes were washed and put away, the little boys were readied for bed. Dad sat reading the paper, and Katie was upstairs to have her private time with her mom. This left Cara with the usual empty feelings of not really belonging, of not knowing what to do with herself. She was too tired to read a book; plus, there were none that interested her at the moment. There were puzzles, but her mind was just too spent to take up a challenge. Going to bed early wasn't an option since she didn't want to interrupt the routine upstairs.

She quietly went into the kitchen and sat at the table, wondering what was to become of her. The room was dark except for some evening light coming in at the window, and soon her heavy head and eyelids both obliged the command to sleep. Softly her head rested on the table, and, exhausted, she could do nothing else.

When the mother came downstairs, she and the dad enjoyed some alone time, sitting together on the couch in the living room, making small talk, relaxing. Before long they turned out the lights and took to the stairs, thinking all the kids were in bed. They checked on Katie from the door to her room; thinking her asleep, they never noticed that the other side of the bed was empty.

But Katie wasn't asleep. She waited until her parents had gone through their evening preparations. Then, silently going to her door, she waited until she recognized the even breathing that signified her parents were in bed, asleep. Now to find Cara.

Cautiously, she went downstairs. Where would Cara be hiding? The living room was too open. Still, she checked behind furniture, just in case. Maybe she was in the boys' playroom. No. The office? No, Cara would *never* go in there after what had happened earlier. The kitchen, or the family room? She'd check both. Or perhaps the garage. Cara wouldn't be brave enough to go out there by herself, would she? No, not at night, anyway.

Carefully entering the kitchen, Katie spied Cara immediately, sitting on a chair, her head resting on the table, her back to the door. Katie wasn't sure what she was going to do, now that she found her. It wouldn't be good if her mom and dad were awakened and made aware that they had left Cara downstairs when they went to bed. Katie would have to think about this. Her mind was flip-flopping, but she had a few things she wanted to say to Cara, things she and her friend had conjured that afternoon. Maybe it would be best if they went upstairs. Her parents' room was down the hall far enough that they wouldn't hear anything. And she and Cara would both be in bed, where they were supposed to be come morning. Mom and Dad would never know.

Sweetly, she rubbed Cara's back, carefully waking her so there would be no disturbance.

Noiselessly they tip-toed up the steps. In the bedroom, Katie carefully closed the door. While unusual, Cara never noticed – she was so tired and just wanted to go back to sleep. She went to her side of the room to put on pajamas; to her surprise, Katie followed after. Was she going to help her into bed?

But then it came, Katie releasing a barrage of words full of meanness and spite, whispered through hateful, clenched teeth. "I hate you!" she began her venomous tirade. Cara was wide awake now. What was going on? "My momma said you shouldn't have even been born! You're a *mistake*, did you know that? Maybe you should have been *aborted*! That's what I think. Then nobody would have to go through all this!" And with that, Katie pushed Cara's shoulders so she almost fell onto the bed. "Go back to where you came from!" she hissed, then hastened to her side of the bed; she lay down, facing away from Cara, pulling the covers up over her head. The room was dark, the house silent, as Cara held her breath, trying not to give away the terrifying fear that filled her entire being.

Finally, after what seemed like forever, Cara sat down on the bed. Her head ached, her heart was pounding, and her hands were clenched into fists! She had never been talked to this way, and it caught her totally unawares. What was going on? What did it mean, to be 'aborted'? Had she ever heard that word? Judging from the way Katie spoke, it must be something really awful. And what did Katie mean, a 'mistake', 'never been born'?

Then, a small light went on in her head: Cara remembered overhearing her grandparents a while ago, using those same words. When she asked, her mother cried, then became very angry. She never explained what the words meant, only that Cara was to remember how much she was loved, and that she was a gift from God. She ended by saying, "… and God doesn't make mistakes!" As much as Cara wanted to believe that, her mom wasn't here anymore, and there was no one to love her. Who were these people, anyway? And why did the man say he was her father? What did that mean? Was there some 'mistake' she didn't know about?

Maybe the next day she would ask him. Maybe he wouldn't get

angry. But maybe he would. She might want to think about it for a while before causing more problems for herself.

Even though it was already late, it was some time before either girl fell asleep. Katie's bitterness had hit its mark. This girl, Katie thought to herself, was a mistake, her father's. And Cara *never* should have been born. That's what her mother had said. It wasn't right that she had to suffer this girl's presence in their home. Whatever had happened, Cara had to go. And Katie would do her best to make it happen.

CHAPTER 10

MORE REALITIES OF HOME

The next morning the girls were awakened at the usual time. Since neither had slept well during the night, it took them awhile to get out of bed. When they did, they eyed each other with contempt. Katie had the attitude of ownership, but Cara's stoic demeanor created a strong front that was not to be penetrated.

Upon coming downstairs, the mother announced that, since it was Saturday, she expected everyone to get their jobs done without her having to keep tabs on each little task. This last remark seemed to be aimed at Cara, but Cara wasn't sure why. With her own mom, it was the day to clean everything in order to get ready for Sunday. Cara was used to taking on responsibility, but their apartment was much smaller. Maybe that's what the mother was referring to. Here her tasks were far less: Cara was responsible to get her dirty clothes to the garage for washing, dust the furniture in the living/dining room, clean the downstairs bathroom, and collect all the trash in the house and take it out to the big trash can. To Cara this was a piece-of-cake, and her spirits lifted a bit.

During the last months of her mother's life, she had taken responsibility for doing just about everything in their home. That was until they went back to live with her grandparents full time, just before her mom died. In their apartment, bed sheets were washed almost every day because of her mother's illness. Well, her mom couldn't always get to the bathroom in time. Someone had to clean it up, and her mom was usually too weak to do much. Also, Cara took charge of the dusting, sweeping, and general cleaning, and she made the house shine as much as a nine-year- old could. The days her gramma came to help, Cara received high praise for doing such a fine job.

In this house, it didn't take long to finish her chores, so Cara went to check the laundry. After all, she knew how to hang up clothes so it didn't get wrinkled, match socks, and fold underwear so it would fit nicely in drawers. What she wasn't used to was clothes for a family of five, plus herself. The mother came out to the garage just as Cara had emptied a load from the dryer, beginning to sort it. "What are you doing?" she demanded. "You're getting all the clothes wrinkled!"

Cara was stunned! In trying to be helpful, she was again at the receiving end of a reprimand. "I was only trying to help," she stammered. "I always did the laundry at home. My mom was too sick…"

"Your 'MOM' isn't here, is she? And this isn't her house, is it? It's MY house, and we'll do things the RIGHT way! Do you understand? Now get out of here; go find *someplace*…just keep out of the way!"

What had she done? What was the mother so mad about? Cara's head was spinning, her stomach churning from the verbal onslaught. First Katie, now the mother? What kind of household was this? She hadn't even been here a week, and all she got was anger. Cara slowly backed away, and with the restraint learned from past experiences, she made her way over to the door to the house, her face giving no indication of the hurt the mother had inflicted, the deep-felt injury she had received. Then something caught her eye. Over in another corner there seemed to be a darkened space where a small girl could hide, if she needed to. Some boxes needed to be rearranged, but with them she could build a wall behind which she could make a very private haven. She slipped back there instead of going inside.

When the mother left the garage, Cara snooped around the rest of the area to see what she could use. There was a small desk by the garage door, one you would find in a primary classroom. "Great!" she thought to herself. Taking that, she began to construct her private space, a sanctuary for whenever she needed to keep-out-of-the-way; it would be her safe place, her haven for hiding when there was nowhere else to go. She moved the desk into position and used a smaller, sturdy box as a seat. Other boxes around the front and side would hide her from view as well as provide a back rest. She needed some sort of light. She would look for that later. For now, she had her own space to where she could run away when needed.

It was almost an hour before Cara went back into the house to check the climate. Seems no one had missed her. On the top floor, someone was running the vacuum; she walked around to check the living area. No one was there, either. She wasn't sure where Katie was, but she decided not to look for her. Both boys were taking afternoon naps in the play room, so Cara selected a book off the shelf and took it outside to read. The weather was hot, but there was a breeze coming in off the Gulf; sitting on the front porch was very peaceful. Here, there was no one to abuse her.

Shortly, a neighbor girl came by and greeted her. "You must be Cara."

"That's right. Who are you?"

"I'm Maribelle. Katie and I are best friends. You're the reason I couldn't go with Katie to the theme park, aren't you?" Her introduction was blunt, pointed.

Cara didn't know what to say. "Did she tell you that?"

After a short period of silence while the girls engaged in a sort of staring game, seeing who would lose eye contact first, Cara looked down and continued the conversation. "I'm sorry you couldn't come along. I didn't mean to cause any problems. Seems that's all I do anymore."

Very bluntly, almost without feeling, Maribelle spoke. "Your mother just died, didn't she? That's what Katie said. Why did you come here?"

"I don't know why. They just brought me here. I don't know why." Cara's voice was flat and even without a hint of weakness. She was learning how to deal with confrontation.

A hint of an apology in her voice, Maribelle responded, "Well… I'm sorry. It has to be hard. I don't know what I would do if I lost my momma." Then she added, "Don't you have a dad? Can't he take care of you?"

Cara didn't know quite how to respond to this. "He doesn't know how to," she finally said. That was as close to the truth as she could get. She decided to change the conversation. "Do you go to the same school as Katie?"

The girls had begun to chat when Katie showed up at the door. Totally ignoring Cara, she and Maribelle began talking and then simply walked off, arm-in-arm. A few steps away, they both turned, looked back at Cara, giggled, and then continued off to their own world; secretly, Cara was wishing for a friend with whom she could share things–like how lonely she was, why nobody seemed to love her here, and why this was her home now.

As her mind was pondering her situation, the father drove up into the driveway. He was just coming home from work, whatever it was that he did. He saw Cara sitting on the porch and came over to talk with her. "Cara, what are you doing out here? Enjoying this hot afternoon?" There was a pause as Cara just looked at the father. "Is anything wrong?"

"No." Then she looked down as if holding his gaze was too confrontational. Finally, she spoke: "Can I ask you a question?"

Somewhat cautiously, the father nodded yes.

Looking up at him squarely, she softly ventured into the unknown. "Why did you bring me here?"

More than anything, the father wanted to be honest with this child. What could he say without opening a door that he wanted to keep tightly shut? It was several seconds before he found his voice.

"Cara," he began softly, "I need to take responsibility for you, now that your mother is…gone. The only way I can do that is by bringing you here to live."

"But why? I don't understand. Why do you have to take responsibility for me?"

Behind them, listening quietly, was the mother. She interjected, "Yes, dear, why is that? Or do you want me to explain it to her?"

"Maggie…." he said; then abruptly rising, he went into the house, taking Maggie by the arm and speaking to her in a hushed but annoyed manner. Cara was again left without answers. Eventually, she knew she would find out. She sat for a few minutes more before going into the house. The two adults were in the study, and she easily made her way to her secret place to be left alone.

CHAPTER 11

DEALING WITH CHANGE

Shortly, she heard the front door close and someone drive off in the van. The footsteps inside were too heavy to be anyone but the dad, so Cara quietly sneaked inside with the hope of continuing the conversation with him. To her surprise, she found him playing with the two boys. They wanted to go outside, but the dad was trying to interest them in some of their toys, explaining that it was just too hot to be outside. At first, no one saw Cara standing in the doorway to the playroom; when she was noticed, Jacob ran to her and took her hand. "Come on, Cara; play with us."

Cara smiled, and with a nod from the dad, she came in and sat down with them. "What do you want to play?" she asked.

"Let's play 'build 'em and knock 'em down'!" Jacob replied enthusiastically.

"What's that game?" the father asked, intrigued with the way it sounded.

Cara cautiously explained how it worked; her compatriots began to demonstrate. As the first building was knocked down, the boys shouted with such glee. Cara looked at the dad to catch his reaction, ready to defend the boys. To her amazement, he was all smiles, as if he was truly enjoying the activity. "Let's see how high we can make the next building before we knock it down," he said.

They continued to play the game, each time making the structure different in some way, and finding unique methods to knock it down. Before long, the boys and the dad were in a tangle of arms, wrestling, laughing, and teasing. Cara had never imagined that the dad could be so much fun. She sat back and smiled, probably the first time since she had left her grandparents.

Then he grabbed her arm and dragged her into the mix. She was actually giggling as the dad tickled first one child, then another, making silly faces, and laughing right along with them. Then, and so suddenly, they heard the screen door slam shut. "Quick!" the dad whispered. "Clean up this mess! I'll head mom off to the kitchen."

Too late. She was standing in the doorway to the room, arms loaded with grocery bags, a look of horror on her face. "Clean up this mess! Dan! I want to see you in the kitchen! Now!" And with that, she stomped away.

The dad shook his head gently, motioned for us to straighten the room, and followed his wife. Even with the door closed, it was evident that both adults were angry for the second time that day. About what, Cara didn't know. She decided that, most likely, some of it was because of the mess they had made. She and the boys straightened up the play room as good as new, as the boys said. Then she got them to bring her a book and sat on the floor between them, looking at the pictures, making up stories, and trying to look innocent. The boys knew the routine: they apparently had figured out the necessity of portraying a blameless demeanor for the sake of their parents. Well, for their mom, anyway.

The rest of the afternoon was pretty quiet. Chores were all done in silence, with little speaking or exchange of information. Cara noticed, furthermore, that no one would look at anyone, like they were all angry. Even Katie, who had been gone for most of the afternoon, kept her head down and said nothing. Cara decided to avoid eye contact with everyone as well. Whatever was happening, she wanted no part of it. Supper, which was a store-bought pizza, was subdued…except for the two little boys. They ate their pizza, then once again resurrected their new game, using the paper plates and plastic glasses as toys. Mom's glaring had little effect, which made her even more on edge.

"Well, you can get them ready for bed tonight since you seem to have a handle on their behavior!" At that, the dad actually picked up both boys, one under each arm, and hauled them upstairs.

Katie actually laughed at them until she caught her mom frowning at her. "I'll help clean up the supper, mom, if you have anything else you need to finish yet. Cara can help me, can't you Cara?"

Katie's voice was slick with sarcasm, but Cara was up and out of the kitchen before Katie finished what she was saying. She was hoping she could go into the garage, to her secret place, but the doorway was in the kitchen. If anyone witnessed her going out there, it would bring a barrage of unwanted questions, and she was not going to let anyone in on her plans.

Maybe, she thought, she could hide in the boys' playroom where she could wait for the dad to come back downstairs. She was hopeful of continuing the conversation that had begun on the front porch, the one before the mom interrupted.

Cara ducked into the small room just as the mother left the kitchen and went to the office. Good, Cara thought. Now to catch the dad after he put the two boys to bed.

It seemed an eternity before he made his way down the steps. She made a beeline to intercept him, but the mother came out of the office just as quickly; Cara ducked for cover back in the playroom. The two adults exited into the kitchen; it wasn't long before Cara heard overtones of heated conversations between the mother, the dad, and even Katie.

So much for that, Cara mused. No way was she going to put herself into that melee. And while part of her wanted to wait to try to talk to the dad, part of her knew she was not going to get any further information tonight. Best to just give up...for the time being, anyway.

Might as well head upstairs, she decided. It would be good if she could make it into bed without another ambush from Katie. Stealthily she moved up the steps. No one followed, and, checking on the two little boys, she knew by the even sounds of their breathing that they were already asleep. Good.

Having the bedroom to herself, Cara decided to try to organize her own items. Katie had not given her any place for this, but, in snooping around, Cara noticed an empty drawer which seemed perfect for the small amount of items she owned. Carefully, she put all her freshly washed items into the empty space.

Perfect, she thought to herself. "I might as well keep things organized. No telling how long I'll have to live here." And the sadness she was working to keep at bay crept into her heart. Again. Sitting on the edge of the bed, she pondered her situation as best she could. There simply were no answers. It was as if a dark pallor was enveloping her along with the room.

"I'm not going down that road! It doesn't help! Change the picture!" she forcefully told herself.

Cara's mom had said that, reminding her it doesn't help to focus on what's wrong. "Let God take that," she had said. "Instead, focus on His love, and what He has already done; let His love flow over you, not your sadness."

It took her awhile before she was able to do that. Then she remembered it was Saturday night; she could take a bath and wash her hair and be out of everyone's way in the morning. Well, she assumed so, anyway. Since bedtime for her and Katie was perhaps an hour away, she could get cleaned up and into bed in plenty of time.

Wet hair? Well, she would dry it as best she could. Maybe there was even a hair dryer she could use.

After filling the tub with water, she allowed herself the luxury of soaking. Nice, she thought. As the warm water enveloped her, her thoughts drifted away to other times, other places, like her grandparents', where she was even allowed some foaming bath salts. Then, tears began to invade her privacy again, and the bath came to a quick end. She dried herself quite thoroughly and allowed herself to use the hair dryer hanging on a hook by the sink.

A knock on the door surprised her. "Cara?" It was the mother. "What are you doing?"

Cara quickly put on her pajamas, saying, "I just took a bath. I'm almost done. I wanted to be out of everyone's way in the morning. Is this okay? I used Katie's hair dryer."

There was a brief silence before the mother spoke again, her voice trailing behind her as she walked away. "Fine. Just be sure you clean up the room."

Cara shook her head. Of course she would clean up the room! Well, at least she wasn't in trouble. It would have been nice though if the mother had said, "Good idea!" or something like that. And she wondered what her grandmother would have thought of this woman. "Ever notice how thorns grow on roses? As pretty as the flowers may be, don't be careless or you'll get pricked!" Yes, she was the mother in this home, and to be respected; but she had a lot of thorns! Just stay out of her way.

Cara quietly made her way back to the bedroom. She still had the room to herself; she climbed into bed, enjoying the privacy while she could. As she thought about the day, she decided to focus on the good things that had happened, pushing the negatives out of her mind as quickly as they tried to invade. She began her mental list:

Being able to help with the housework had brought a sense of belonging.

Finding a "private place" in the garage was huge!

Maybe the dad was ready to talk with her. He seemed like it.

Her list was interrupted as she heard the door open. It was Katie. There was no way Cara was going to let her know she was still awake. She lay facing the wall, keeping her breathing even.

Katie proceeded to move around the room without any pretense that she acknowledged Cara's presence, or even that Cara might be asleep. She opened and closed drawers, slammed the bedroom door shut, and without any care, pretty much just dropped herself onto the bed. Obviously she wanted Cara to be awake. Cara did not oblige.

Then, hissing through clenched teeth, Katie aimed her rifle at Cara, hoping to rile her enough to cause pain. "I know you're not sleeping! No one wants you here, do you understand? Go back to your dead mama!" Cara gave her no response. With her head on the pillow, covers tucked under her chin, she was able to ignore the bullets, mentally continuing her list and reveling in the fun she had had with the – no, *her* – dad. For the first time since arriving, she actually fell soundly asleep and slumbered through the night.

CHAPTER 12

NEW UNDERSTANDINGS

Cara awoke to her first Sunday morning in this new house. After breakfast, they all dressed up, got into the van, and drove to church. Cara was glad she had bathed the night before; there would not have been time otherwise. Everyone did their own thing, and Cara was ready when everyone else was. The drive to church was less than 15 minutes, and everyone scurried out of the van as if they were late. Katie actually grabbed Cara's arm and led her to Sunday school, while the mother took the two boys with her to another room filled with noisy little children. The father seemed to disappear; to where, Cara didn't know. Maybe he didn't go to church.

An hour later, Katie and Cara joined the mother and the two little boys; they took their places in church, sitting more toward the back. Confused, Cara tried to get the mother's attention, wanting to ask where dad was, but instead she got scolded: "Behave! Don't embarrass your father!" What that meant, Cara had no idea. One more piece to add to her puzzle. Then, as the first hymn was being sung, she saw a man in a white robe walk down the center aisle and take his place on the top step in the front. The song over, he turned and faced the congregation.

"Good morning," he intoned, a bright smile on his face. Cara couldn't believe this; it was her father, and he was the pastor! *Her father was the pastor of this church!* She wondered if her mom and grandparents knew this. Why hadn't they ever told her? They had never spoken about him, and she just assumed he had died or something.

This made her begin to wonder even more: what had happened when she was born? If he was really her father, why had he left them? Then it came to her: If Katie was a year older than she, and she had a different mom than her own, he must have already had a family. Had they divorced, then gotten back together sometime? More questions. Cara still didn't quite get it all, but some parts of the puzzle had just shown up.

After the service, they waited for dad to finish visiting; that was part of his job, she was told. The mother, she found out, taught a class of three-year-olds at the school that was part of the church. So, before leaving, they stopped in her classroom to pick up some work she wanted to complete at home. She needed to get a head start, she had said, and Cara helped carry construction paper to the van. Now Cara knew, she thought to herself, where the desk in garage had come from. What other treasures could be there?

The trip home included a stop for breakfast, which Cara really didn't understand since they had already eaten one at home. This family had many surprises! Some were good, some were puzzling, and some just plain strange!

Finally, back at the house, Cara learned more of the Sunday routine. It was a day of rest for dad: he started the afternoon watching a baseball game, one of the few times the TV was on, but fell asleep before too long; the little boys pestered Katie until she had enough of them and left the house to find her friend; Cara took over playing with the boys until they, too, nodded off, heavy eyelids getting the best of them. The mother, on the other hand, who always seemed to be busy, had disappeared into the office, not to be seen until it was time to put some supper together.

Not knowing what else to do, Cara went to her garage haven where she could be alone and not disturb anyone. She sat, leaning against the wall. How strange, she thought to herself. This house doesn't have a "family"; it just has people who are related. What happened to them? All they do is live in the same building. Not like she and her mom and grandparents; they did things together, like cooking, baking, taking care of the lawn, and sometimes even playing games.

Cara remembered helping her grandpa make a planter for the front of the house – holding boards as he cut them, painting the box after they had hammered it together, and choosing and putting in the colorful plants that made the porch look nice. Gramma was teaching her to crochet, but she wasn't quite getting the hang of it. With a little more practice, gramma had said, she'd do fine; she just had to keep working at it. If they ever just sat around, they'd get out a board game or a deck of cards, or just tell stories; whether they were true or made up didn't matter; they took turns entertaining each other. At the very least, there was conversation, each recalling some person they ran into, or something going on at church.

Cara missed all this. Someday, she decided, she would have her own family and home, and it would be full of love and happiness, and the people would like being part of it. What to do right now, though?

Sitting in her corner and looking at her boxes, it didn't take Cara very long to decide what to do with her space: she would decorate it. She began exploring some of the better-kept boxes. Did these people keep anything that she could use? Eventually, she discovered a box that contained partially used school supplies – construction paper, drawing paper, markers, pencils, some Scotch tape, a pair of scissors, and some stickers. "Perfect!" she thought to herself. Certainly no one would miss a few of these items – the box looked like it had been here for ages. "What a gold mine!" she almost said out loud. And the decorating began.

"I need happy shapes," she decided; hearts, flowers, trees, smiling faces, and little children having fun. Ideas began to form in her mind, and before long she had sketched out what would go on each box. One, the biggest box, would have a playground with children doing various activities such as swinging, playing catch, and jumping rope; on a second box, a smaller one, a smiling teacher would be helping a small child; another box would have a lot of trees with children climbing and playing under them. Maybe there would be room for another scene with a field, a picnic table, and a water fountain. A sign would be put over the top of the biggest box that would say, "The Happy Playground".

Her ideas now organized, Cara began construction of the biggest scene. Adeptly she sketched and cut out each person, added different colors of paper for clothes, and drew faces and other details with a thin marker she had found. Her characters came alive in her mind; she even began to name them and visually placed them in position. When everything for this picture was finished, she carefully used the tape to attach them. The result was amazing!

Cara's creation was beautiful! Her happy playground had begun to take shape.

By now, she decided, it must be late in the day, and she didn't want any more problems…if she could help it. It was time to go in. Carefully she left the safety of her shelter, moved the boxes to make them look unobtrusive, and went to the door to the house. Hearing nothing, she gradually opened the door and quietly slipped inside. She began making her way to the door that led to the dining room when it opened. It was the mother! Now what?

"Cara, what are you doing in the kitchen?"

"I just wondered what we're having for supper. I thought I could help."

"Hmmph!" the mother replied. "Okay. Do you know which bowls are for soup? They're next to the cereal bowls, only bigger. Get down four of those and two cereal bowls for the boys. And don't drop any! I put some stew in the crock pot this morning, so we'll have that and some fresh fruit."

Cara was amazed. She was actually allowed to help. "Do you want some bread or crackers to go with that?" she asked.

Again the mother paused, looking at Cara with part scowl, part annoyance. Finally, she said, "Sure. And get some peanut butter and jelly, too, if I know my two boys."

Shortly, everything was ready, the troops were called, and the family ate the third meal of the day. It was very uneventful, with little conversation. The mother's mind was on her work, Katie acted as if she was totally bored with everyone, and the dad was in his own world. Cara observed each person surreptitiously. So, this was what Sunday is like around here? At least she had her own private place now, she thought to herself. "I can escape...when I need to."

Afterward, the mother went back to the office and left the clean-up in everyone else's hands. Dishes were washed and put away, everyone doing their part, and the family ended up in the living room where they watched a video. It was Sunday night. Family time, dad said.

Well, Cara thought, they *were* doing something together.... minus the mother, of course.

Shortly, a feeling of tiredness hit the two little boys, and dad asked the girls to help get the boys upstairs and to bed. Each girl took one boy, and they carried them to their room. It seemed that Katie was still in her own world – there was no conversation between them, and when dad came up shortly, she went back downstairs.

Cara picked up on the opportunity to confront her dad with her queries while they were still somewhat fresh in her mind and she had him all to herself. She didn't know he was a pastor, she said first; then, she continued, "Why do you say you're my father? And if you are, why did you leave us?"

She had caught him off guard, and he quickly brushed her off, saying he would tell her the story when she was older and able to understand it better. Cara knew this was an adult's way of saying, "I don't want to talk about it." So she let it go, helped with the two boys, and decided to head for bed herself. What else was there to do? As intuitive as Cara was, she knew it wouldn't be long before she had all the pieces together. Then she'd face these adults and make them 'fess up; at least, that was the plan. For now, she had her "Happy Playground" to dream about.

So ended the first Sunday in this new environment. Cara took care of her bedtime preparations, carefully putting her own things in order. By the time Katie came to bed, Cara was sound asleep, and the household was settled for the night.

CHAPTER 13

THE DIFFERENCE

With one week until school would start, Cara vacillated between excited expectations and fearful imaginings. In the past, Cara would look forward to seeing her friends again every day. Here, she had no friends. She didn't know anyone. At all. Before, a new school year meant new beginnings with fun things to learn. Here, she imagined herself experiencing untold difficulties in adjusting. Furthermore, she had never concerned herself with the clothes she would wear. Poor as they were, she got what was needed from the local resale store; the clothes were always new to her. Here, she would wear uniforms. She wasn't sure about that, not sure how she would look. She might even look weird, somehow.

Her dad stayed home from work that week – said he was taking one of his vacation weeks. This way he would stay with the three – now four – children, while the mother would go to school to get her classroom ready. She also made visits to all the families with children in her class. Cara hoped the mother would be nicer to them than she was to her. She had a hard time imagining the mother as a teacher. Maybe she was better with the three-year-olds.

Cara enjoyed the days with her dad. He had fun doing things with his kids, making a game out of the work that was on his to-do list. There were charts for things that needed doing at the house, and they all worked together to get them done. The list included cleaning out the flower beds, raking leaves, straightening and cleaning out the refrigerator, and other summer projects dad assigned on an individual basis. The best part was when the work was finished: Dad took his work force for ice cream…or some kind of sweet treat. Dad called it a reward for good work.

On Thursday dad took the four kids shopping. They all had to get school supplies, he said. Each child had a list of items required by the homeroom teacher. To Cara, this was all very strange. First of all, she had never seen a list of school supplies this long. Secondly, as far as she knew, no teacher of hers in the past had a list of required items. Either that, or her mom could never afford to buy all the things on the list. She could hear her mother now: "Most likely you'll lose half this stuff before you need it, and the rest of it you'll probably never use. Let's just wait."

Not so with this school or this family. If it was on the list, it had to be bought, and obviously it would be needed. Cara found this extravagance unbelievable. And strange.

"What a bunch of loot," she exclaimed excitedly when everything was laid out on the kitchen table.

Each child also had a new book bag. Well, Cara's was Katie's old one from last year. But it was new to Cara, and that was fine with her. No use throwing out something that still has a lot of good use in it, as her mother used to say. Katie, on the other hand, was amazed. She would never accept anything that was used. The items all were packed away, some in the book bags to go with them to school on Monday, and others to be stored for later use as needed. Now Cara knew why the materials that she used to decorate her boxes were in the garage.

Another chore was presented on Friday. Katie got out all her uniforms from the year before. Any with stains or holes were to be thrown out, but the usable items were to be washed. If they fit Cara, she would get them. Any that didn't would be donated to the resale shop housed in the school office. Cara had never seen this kind of clothing, let alone witnessed it being worn at school. Each item Katie discarded, Cara was quick to pick up.

"What's wrong with this one? So what if it has a hole in it. That can be fixed real easy." Or, "This stain isn't that bad. A little stain remover and good old-fashioned elbow grease, and it'll be just fine."

Katie and her dad watched as Cara took charge of the project. All the really good items, which were only a few, were put aside for Cara. The other uniform parts were mended, treated for stains, added to the wash, and then double checked for usability. Admittedly, some still had to be rejected; but, when finished, there was a total of 6 completely usable uniforms, tops and bottoms. Cara was beaming. Why, she would be proud to wear them.

Katie, of course, would be getting all new uniforms for school as she did each year. For one thing, she had grown into the next size. But, more than that, she would never wear last year's clothes. That's what the term "used" meant, and that was not part of their life-style. "Doing your best starts with looking your best." Her mom had instilled that in Katie's mind.

Both little boys would be going to pre-school this year, and while they didn't wear uniforms at their age, it was still necessary to make sure there were enough clothes to make it through the week. New clothes would be bought as needed, of course, but getting everything laid out and checked for the beginning of the school year was also on the day's agenda. Once again, Cara took charge, quickly figuring out what was needed. Items were washed, mended, and ironed, if needed, to make a good impression. While there were enough shirts for little Sammy, Jacob would need several new ones; and, both boys needed new shorts, the old ones were beyond looking presentable, as determined by Cara.

Dad and Katie just looked at each other. Something that would have caused multiple discussions and taken them all day was finished by early afternoon, thanks to Cara's input and energy. Who was this little girl? Even Katie was softer to her on this day, amazed at what Cara could do. Furthermore, since there was time left in the schedule, they all went shopping for the little boys' clothes – stopping for the obligatory ice cream on the way home, of course.

Mom finally got home for a pizza supper – she had picked up a couple on the way, concerned about the amount of work that lay ahead of her yet. With four children to get ready for school on Monday, plus her own items, her stress level was at the roof. And, she thought to herself, who knows what actually had gotten done today? She didn't depend on her husband to rally the troops because he probably had no idea what to do. And while Katie would be helpful, she knew it was beyond the two of them.

Also, she lamented, there was Cara – not only one more person, but she brought too much baggage to the family. This wasn't working. Cara didn't belong with them – too many problems for Katie as well as everyone else. It was definitely time to discuss this with her husband.

Coming in the front door, dad immediately rushed to help unload her items, especially the pizza. They were hungry. He had cut up some fruit to go with it, and each of them already had their drink. Supper was on the table. "Let's eat" was foremost on everyone's mind. Putting everything else in the office, the mother joined them in the kitchen. She was weary.

"So, how did it go around here today? What has to get done yet?" Mom's voice sounded somewhat accusatory in tone.

"Nothing." Dad was quick to the point.

"Really? Everyone's clothes are all ready to go…for the week. Washed, mended, new items bought for the boys…uniforms sorted and ready for the resale store…

"Maggie, everything is done. Just as you wanted. All four kids' clothes are…ready! We got it done, just as you wanted." The smile on dad's face spread to all four kids; the mother was still incredulous.

"We'll see." It wasn't that she didn't believe them. She didn't trust what Dan was saying. There was no way it could be so easy. "Finish supper first. Then, I'll take a look."

Mom would have the final say – it had to meet her criteria. Looking around the table, she noticed all four children were smiling at her. Something was up. What had they done? Her curiosity could last no longer. She abruptly left the table and went upstairs. Everyone else stayed put, waiting for the result.

Fifteen minutes later, mom appeared in the doorway to the kitchen. Her face all smiles, she declared, "I don't believe it! How did you get all that together? Everything is perfect! I don't have to do a thing! Wait a minute! Who came in here and did this for you? I know none of you could have gotten everything organized and looking like that. Who was it?"

Grinning, dad looked over at Cara, but it was Katie who announced the news. "You won't believe this mom, but Cara was the one. She figured out what had to be done and put us all to work. Thanks to her, everything on your list is finished."

Mom's jaw dropped. "Cara? When did you learn to do….all that?" mom asked, waving her arm and pointing upstairs. "Never mind. I'm just glad it's done. Thank you, everyone. I know it was a *group* project." Cara felt the arrow that was meant for her, but she let it bounce right off. This had been a good day, and she had been part of the family. No one could take that from her.

After the supper was over and the table cleared, the mother went to her office to work. Dad and the four kids went for a walk together, heading for the small neighborhood park where the boys always wanted to go to play. Cara was walking behind everyone, feeling pretty good about all the work they had done together. Then, Katie was at her side. Cara smiled a little, thinking that maybe things were starting to change. Katie stared for a minute, then said, "You think this makes any difference? This still isn't your home. We just used you today, that's all." Then she walked ahead, taking her dad's hand as the two boys walked ahead of them.

This startled Cara. What a strange family! How could Katie be so nice to her at supper, and then be so hurtful now? What was up with her? Why couldn't she see that they could at least be friends? Her heart sank. "I don't really want to be here, anyway," she thought to herself, and again she knew that she had to find a way to run away, to go back home. And soon. Before school started. And if they don't want her there, she'd find someplace else to go. She just needed a plan.

CHAPTER 14

SHOPPING WITH
THE MOTHER

While Saturday was usually reserved to clean the whole house, this one was different. The mother was home, and everything had to be double checked for school for next week. Even the two little ones received final inspections. Everything had to pass the mother's scrutiny. Plus, the mother had made a comment that the girls needed new clothes. She, especially, needed new outfits for the classroom, and Katie had outgrown most of her casual clothes. It was decided that they would take Cara along as most of her clothes were too ragged for this family. And, she, too, had outgrown most of what she had brought along.

By early afternoon, troop assignments had been laid out – dad had to babysit the boys – and Cara, Katie, and the mother boarded the family van and set out for sights unknown, at least as far as Cara was concerned. The first stop was to deliver discarded clothing to the re-sale shop.

Upon entering the store, Cara immediately felt as though she was greeting an old friend. Knowing that she was to get some new clothes, she began looking around, making her way to the racks of Girls' Clothes. She began rummaging through the assemblage of usable items – jeans, t- shirts, blouses, dresses, etc. Her careful selections included two pairs of jeans, one pair of dressy pants, two blouses, and a jacket. Just for fun, she threw in a pair of sandals, feeling fairly sure they would be rejected. Adding the cost of all items, the total would be close to $15.00.

Katie and her mom had not ventured farther than the front drop-off area. Cara approached, head held high because of the great bargains she had acquired. Excitedly, she presented each item with a comment on its usefulness, finally asking in all boldness, "Can I get these?"

"Let's see," the mother said, winking at her daughter and looking over Cara's choices. "Yes, these will do. How are you going to pay for them?"

This caught Cara off guard. Her countenance fell. "I don't know," she said softly. "I don't have any money. Can I work it off somehow?"

Katie and her mom both laughed at this. "Oh, Cara. We're just teasing you. I'll buy this for you…if you're sure this is what you want. We're doing some more shopping. Don't decide later to change your mind…"

"Oh, no, I won't! These are really nice bargains."

The three of them exited the store, Cara confidently toting her bag of new clothes.

The only thing she couldn't understand was why neither Katie nor her mom had bought anything. Hadn't they gone out to shop for clothes? How could they pass up such good deals?

Their next stop was a huge shopping mall, the kind with all the big name stores. Cara had never been to one of these kinds of places. In fact, whenever she and her mom and grandparents drove past one, they would joke about all the rich people giving away their money to keep up appearances, whatever that meant. They would all laugh and pretend to be snobs handing out money right and left.

Here, however, as they drove up to one of the entrances and parked, Cara kept her mouth shut. She was truly amazed by what she saw, her eyes darting here and there, sometimes focusing on a particular nuance of the place. The decorative walkways with hanging flowers and manicured gardens, the massive stone buildings with glass encased show rooms, and the constant parade of people flowing throughout the confines of the mall were more than her senses could observe as they moved through it. The mother had to take her hand for fear of losing her in the crowd.

Once inside, they rode on an eggs-later, or something like that. At the top, they made their way to a really big, fancy store and went inside to the Young Ladies' Department. They passed several racks of clothing with SALE signs, most of the prices much more than the total amount they had spent at the re-sale shop. Cara was taken to an area where there were some chairs and was told to sit down and stay there until they came to get her. No problem there, she thought to herself. She wouldn't be able to find her way out of here even with a trail of bread crumbs. Furthermore, she had seen nothing that interested her. She had made her selections and was totally satisfied.

Surveying the immediate area, she noticed a sign on a doorway not far from her chair. The words Dressing Rooms over the entrance puzzled her for a moment. "Huh," she thought to herself, "they even have special rooms you can buy to get dressed in. But how do you get them home?" The strangeness of the store was more than she could fathom.

After what seemed like a long wait, Katie and her mom showed up with armloads of clothing. They passed by Cara without saying a word and went inside the dressing rooms. Sometime later they returned, not carrying anything. This puzzled Cara: What did they do with the armloads of clothes they had taken inside? It wasn't long before the scene was repeated. This time, however, they came out with a few of the items. This was all very confusing.

"What happens with the rest of the clothes?" she whispered to a girl sitting next to her who looked much older.

"What clothes?"

"People go in there with lots of clothes. Sometimes they come back out with nothing, and sometimes they come out with something. What happens to the rest of it?"

"They leave it in there."

"But what happens to it? Does it go to another store? Does it go down some special chute for poor people to get?"

"Haven't you ever been in a dressing room before?" The girl sounded a little flustered. "You go in there, try on the clothes you picked, and what you don't want you leave in the room."

This made no sense to Cara; she still had no answer to her question. Oh, well, she decided; it wasn't worth pursuing since she probably would never shop in one of these places ever again. At least she hoped not. This was not her.

Before long, Katie and her mother came to retrieve Cara. With armloads of items, they went to a check-out station to purchase what they had chosen. Cara's mouth dropped open when she saw the total on the cash register; she immediately worked to hide her amazement, not wanting to give Katie and her mom any kind of ammunition against her. What she couldn't understand, though, was why they would pay so much for things Katie probably wouldn't wear in a few months. She could hear her own mother saying, "At the rate you're growing, these won't fit you by Christmas anymore, so why pay all that money?"

Leaving the store and the buildings, they quickly found the van and unloaded all their packages. Katie sat in the front seat next to her mother, and Cara sat quietly in her usual spot in the very back, contemplating all that had transpired since they left home. This was a very puzzling family, she decided again. What interested her now was the difference between the world in which she grew up and this new society into which she had been catapulted.

In all innocence, she was totally unprepared for this way of life; it was like living with aliens. However, what she didn't know was that what lay ahead would present even more challenges, more assaults on her naivety.

CHAPTER 15

SUNDAY FUN

The routine from the previous Sunday was pretty much repeated, except that when they got to church, there was no Sunday School. It was the day before school was to start, so everyone was given a reprieve. The family arrived early since Dan was expected to conduct adult Bible class. However, this early arrival caused tension in the family: someone had to look after the kids. Mom had planned to use the time in her classroom. That left it up to Katie to babysit her two brothers, something Katie thought was grossly unfair. Seems there were other friends who had also showed up early, and the three of them already had plans. Cara was willing to take care of the two boys, but she was not sure what she would do with them. They were in their Sunday clothes and could *not* get dirty. So, no playing on the playground.

The situation got worse when more children were dropped off, bringing the total number of orphans to 12. Apparently, the word about "No Sunday School" had not been properly disseminated, and it became evident that something would have to be organized for this motley group. It fell to the mother–after all, she was a teacher–to come up with something. Either that, or let them all run amuck around the church and school grounds, which was something she would not allow.

Begrudgingly, she took them all to her classroom. But just what could she do with such a diverse group? Her frustration was getting the better of her when help came from the most unexpected place: Cara. In a corner of the room, she had found parts of costumes—robes, masks, and other paraphernalia related to drama.

"Can we use these to act out Bible stories?" she quietly asked.

"Well, I guess so. Make sure you put them back where you found them. Don't leave a mess." While the mother was skeptical of allowing it, playing with the items might give her a reprieve from producing some sort of activity for them. On the other hand, Cara thought the mother would be willing to help, and she was surprised when she found herself in charge of the project. She jumped right in, gathering the group on the floor in a corner. By the time they were all seated, Cara had her plan.

"Do you remember the story of Moses?" she asked. All the hands went up at once. She continued, "Let's act out the crossing of the Red Sea. Who wants to be Moses?"

Several hands went up, and she gave a costume to the biggest kid. He also got to handle a stick that was to be his staff. "No hitting anyone! That's what God gave him, remember? So, be careful with it." Cara gave orders with a sense of authority, and the kids responded accordingly.

Eventually, she had everyone in a costume, playing an important part of the story. With Cara's dramatic telling of the story, they were to pantomime their parts. And, if they knew what was going on, they could even speak some lines. Cara had to take the part of pharaoh's army crossing the sea because nobody wanted to drown. That would end their participation.

Moses led everyone, so he went first, ordering people around, making sure they got through the sea on dry ground. As the water started to come back, made very real by Cara's telling and the sound effects she encouraged, he made sure they were all safely behind him.

It was great! This was fun, Cara thought to herself. Sunday School should always be like this.

The next part of the journey was to go to Mt. Sinai. The older students remembered the problems they had on the way – no water, no food, and arguing! So they acted out each part of the story, telling how God provided what was needed, until they finally arrived at their destination where God gave Moses the Ten Commandments. At that point, Cara decided it was time to sit. They had been marching long enough!

But what to do next, she thought to herself? Some kids began talking and rough housing, and Cara was at a loss as to what to do. From behind them she heard the mom ask, "Who knows why Moses led the Children of Israel out of Egypt?" And so began a discussion of the story. Everyone wanted to tell what he or she knew, and several times the mother had to get them all under control as well. But she did. And Cara felt good about how everything came together, especially how the mother had honored her with the responsibility.

They finished with a song, and the mother led them in a short prayer. Parents were already at the door to pick up the kids. The 45 minutes had gone fast, and the mother had actually been able to organize some material to take home and work on there, thanks to Cara's leadership.

"Cara, that was very helpful," she said. "Where did you come up with that idea?"

Cara's reply was not what the mother wanted to hear. "I used to help my mom in Sunday School all the time. We did stuff like this…" Noticing the look on the mother's face made her stop in mid-sentence.

"I don't want to hear about your mother, do you understand?" The mother's words were as clipped and angry as any that Katie had spoken. Once again, Cara shored herself up in protective armor, showing no emotion, no visible response. Inside, she was reeling!

What was wrong with this family? Why did they treat her this way? Looking at Katie, Cara noticed a smirk on her face as if to say, "I told you so!"

Closing up the classroom, they all made their way into the church; Cara had regained the stoicism that had saved her many times. Even being in church did not make a chink in her armor today. She made it through the service and kept her demeanor in place for the rest of the morning, including the stop for breakfast and the ride home. Once there she made a beeline upstairs to change her clothes, her main goal to stay out of Katie's way.

From there she was able to steal quietly into the garage, to her private haven. But nothing here drew her mind away from the distress of the morning. Instead, rebel tears came flooding down her face. She couldn't help it. What had she done that made this woman hate her so much?

CHAPTER 16

ON BEING THE NEW GIRL

At this point, she needed most of all to just get out of the house, away from this family, this existence, and just go somewhere. She left the garage by the side entrance, being quiet not to alert anyone to her absence. What would they care, anyway? It was Sunday. It didn't seem to matter what anyone did, so they wouldn't miss her until supper. Maybe she would be back by then, and maybe not.

Her footsteps took her to the park, the only place she had been where they hadn't taken the car. No one else was using the playground, so it was all hers. She sat on a swing, feeling her loneliness like a heavy anchor on her heart. If she could just find one friend, one person to confide in, one person with whom she could laugh and play. Otherwise, she would just have to run away. If she left now, no one would miss her for several hours. By then it would be too late, and she would be too far away for them to find her. Maybe someone would give her a ride…somewhere! But what if she were kidnapped? Would anyone miss her? Random thoughts rampaged through her mind, each one leading to a sad, even more miserable ending.

Cara had become so lost in her musings that she was unaware of three girls who had walked up behind her. While she didn't know them, they knew who she was, and with rough hands they grabbed her and threw her to the ground. Cara screamed, once, before she caught herself, and quickly stood up. "Who are you? What do you want?"

"Just playing. Can't you take a joke?" The girl who spoke seemed bigger than the other two and was obviously the leader. "You're the preacher's kid, aren't you? The new one he brought here after your mother died."

Cara kept her thoughts to herself, not allowing her emotions to come to the surface. "Like I said, who are you? What do you want?" Her insides were quaking, but Cara was not one to back down from a bully. And she had seen enough of them in her short life. They always had something to say about her mother.

"I'm Britney. And you'll be seeing all three of us tomorrow when school starts. We're all in the same class."

"Yeah. We just thought we'd get to know you ahead of time. I'm Aubrie."

"My name's Caroline." The introductions over, all three girls began to crash into Cara's space, again pushing her until she fell down. "Just remember who's in charge, got it?" Then, laughing, they ran off as quickly as they had come.

Cara brushed herself off. Now, more than before, it was evident that she had to run away. No place was safe. Unfortunately, the questions still remained: where would she go, and how would she get there? Slowly, she padded her way back to the house, working to get her insides to settle down, her mind wandering in circles. What an awful day this was turning out to be. Nothing made sense; what was to become of her?

Quietly she entered the house through the kitchen. No one was in there. Checking the rest of the house, she found dad sleeping on the couch, the mother working in the office, and the two little boys taking naps on the floor of the playroom. Listening, she heard Katie upstairs, talking on a phone to someone, probably her friend Maribelle. Now what do I do, she said to herself. Might as well sit down in the family room. That way someone would be watching the television that was broadcasting the afternoon baseball game. "Maybe I can learn about baseball," she thought to herself. And she sat in a chair, staring at the screen, not really looking at anything.

Hearing some movement in the playroom, Cara decided to check on the two boys. They were both awake, but an argument had ensued about their toys. They both noticed Cara at the same time, and for the first time all day, she felt loved. Sitting down with them, they both vied for her lap; knowing this noise would bring unwanted attention from someone, she stood up, took their hands, and began to tip toe around the room. "Let's go outside," she whispered, and the boys followed her lead and tip toed through the living room, through the kitchen, and out the back door.

"What shall we play?" Cara asked them. They had no idea. The yard, although immense, was just a lot of space with no swings, toys, or equipment. Struck with an idea, she called out, "Let's play tag. I'm it!" And with that, she began to chase first Jacob, then Samuel. She could have caught either one, but what was the fun in that?

Before long, Cara stopped short; she was out of breath. Both boys took delight in taunting her to continue the game, and Cara finally grabbed ahold of them; all three rolled around on the grass, laughing and teasing, arms and legs thrashing all about, tickling each other and just plain having fun. Cara thought that by now someone, disturbed by the noise, would have come to check on them. Didn't happen. Maybe they had become invisible. Or something.

She and the two boys spent more than an hour playing, exploring the yard, making up stories and acting them out, or just sitting and talking. They had no qualms about who she was or why she had come to live with them. She was their playmate, a person who cared about them, and someone who knew how to have fun. And they loved her. Cara had found an oasis in the midst of her loneliness.

Unexpectedly, a call came from the back door. It was Katie telling Cara she had to come help with supper. As Cara went in, Katie proceeded to give her orders, and then went out to bring in the two boys. When she saw the state of their appearance, she burst out in a reprimand that modeled her mother. "Just look at you!" she exclaimed. "Your clothes are all dirty! What's Mother going to say?" And she brought them in and took them upstairs. All the way up, Cara heard Katie fuss at her siblings. How did they get so messy? In their sweaty, dirty condition, they would not be allowed to sit at the supper table with everyone else! They had to change clothes and clean up.

Life was back to normal for this family, Cara thought to herself. How did they get to be this way? At the supper table, however, she kept getting grins from two little boys who really didn't care about being dirty or clean. They had had a good Sunday afternoon, all because of Cara. She smiled back at them. Maybe she would stick around here for the sake of Jacob and Samuel. Maybe they needed her.

Before leaving the table, the mother went over the schedule for the next day, especially the morning when everyone had to be ready and in the van. She would be driving them, but dad would follow in his car. When they arrived, he would make sure everyone got to their particular classrooms. After all, tomorrow was the first day of school, and the mother would have to be in her own classroom right away.

After everything was cleared from the supper table, Katie was allowed a half hour with her friend. Cara felt relieved since this allowed her to go upstairs and get to bed without noticeable incident. She wasn't tired, but she didn't want to face Katie's angst. Cara was amassing too much of her own. Once in bed, she could pretend to be asleep and, hopefully, put off any of Katie's newest tirades. The drama of the day was already at its limit for Cara. She wanted nothing more than a sense of peace.

Unfortunately, sleep would not come, even hours after Katie had come to bed; Cara just couldn't get out of the funk that kept invading her thoughts: the three girls at the playground, the mother's spiteful comments about her mother, and Katie's continual cruel treatment, for no reason, at least none of which Cara was aware. And, in the midst of all this, she started school tomorrow. This was the unknown that undergirded everything else right now. Her turmoil was immense. It all kept playing over and over in her mind; and when she finally fell into an exhausted sleep, she was worn out from mentally reliving all that was wrong in her life. There were simply too many demons.

CHAPTER 17

HANK AND MARION'S DILEMMA

Cara's grandparents had had nothing but Cara on their minds since she had been taken from them. It had already been two weeks, and they thought they would have heard something by now. Each day they had become more and more fretful about her well-being, questioning what they had agreed to. They had known Dan when he was their pastor nine years ago; Maggie, too, for that matter—she had started the pre-school program that was still operating out of their church facilities—but Hank and Marion were full of unrest about the kidnapping of their granddaughter, as they referred to it. Cara didn't know them—her mother had never told Cara anything about her beginnings. How would these two people deal with the past, even convey to Cara what had happened, in such a way that she would feel accepted, even loved?

Their anxiety about calling vacillated between trusting that everything was going fine to feelings of anger over Cara's being taken from them. However, they didn't want to seem like they were meddling. Give them all a chance to get to know each other without interference, they thought. Certainly they would see the goodness in their precious granddaughter; and, with the death of her mother so recent, they would do everything needed to help her through the crisis, wouldn't they? Certainly they would be cognizant of at least this much, of Cara's need for comfort and love.

What bothered them both, however, was Maggie's comment when asked if she and her husband had both agreed to bring Cara into their household. Her response, along with her manner, was disquieting – almost callous. Had she and Dan come to terms in their marriage, or was there still a wedge in their relationship? It almost seemed as such. Perhaps, however, they were just tired from the drive; or, perhaps there were other tensions that Hank and Marion were not privy to, things that would settle down once Cara was actually with them. If not, Cara's life could be miserable.

Hank and Marion had considered both sides, and on several occasions, they were ready to drive to New Port Richie to see for themselves how Cara was doing. They were extremely unsettled, unable to decide if they were over-reacting to their own distresses or if there was real evidence for concern.

There were other matters to consider. Legally, Hank and Marion had no rights to take Cara into their household. The fact that she and her mother had lived with them until Cara was four years old would not matter in a court of law. Her father, on the other hand, did have legal rights to take her. He had sent money for her support throughout her life as well as sharing genetic makeup with her.

If he was abusive, that would be different. But he was well-respected as a man of the cloth, and even in their own church, many people still wished he was their pastor. Even his wife, Maggie, was loved and respected by those who knew her. Young families who had put their trust in her to care for their very young children raved that she was not only responsible, but she had been a competent counselor when they needed direction. Why would the government give custody of Cara to grandparents? This would happen only if there was open agreement, and if all parties concurred. Cara's grandparents doubted this was a viable pathway.

Furthermore, all the qualms they were feeling could be unfounded. Certainly, if the problems were that serious, someone would have called by now. All their consternation, they decided, was without foundation. They were reacting to their own grief—their daughter had died, and their grand-daughter was gone as well. It was best for all involved to move into the future. This included allowing Cara and her new family to become family without intervention from two over-reactive grandparents.

Finally, they settled on a plan. They would call Dan and Maggie, just a thoughtful inquiry as to how everything was going, and did Cara need anything that was left behind. Unfortunately, the phone went to the answering service which wasn't working, or something. It was full, or so the message said. They decided to just let it go, for the time being. Perhaps, they told themselves, Dan didn't answer the phone on a Sunday.

The next day, however, they were adamant about contacting someone. For whatever reason, they were more than concerned. Their anxiety was causing tremendous upset. They each had a strange feeling inside that told them something was wrong. Remembering that school was starting, they decided to try Dan at his church office. If he wasn't there, at least someone could take a message that they had called.

After three rings, the secretary answered; no, Pastor Dan was not in the office, but she could take a message if they wanted to leave one. When Hank identified himself as Cara's grandfather, the secretary responded as if she were talking to an old friend, someone she had known all her life. With that, Hank ventured into his reason for calling—to see how everything was going, and how things were with Cara.

"That's some granddaughter you have!" The secretary's voice was kind and expressive.

She proceeded to tell how Cara had made yesterday's Sunday school class fun and exciting. Seems her own daughter was in attendance, even though Sunday school had been cancelled. Cara had saved the day by organizing everyone to perform the story of Moses and the Israelites leaving Egypt. "Besides getting everyone involved, she had a good lesson. I'm sure Dan and Maggie are enjoying having her. I can give them a message for you…"

Hank decided not to – he and Marion didn't want to appear as if they were interfering. And, if Cara was doing alright, that was their main concern. In fact, he asked her not to even tell Dan they had called. No sense meddling in the family's affairs; someone would certainly call if there were problems.

They also trusted that God was in charge: He knew the future, had it all planned, and held it all in His hands. This included Cara and her new family. While it was difficult to deal with the hardships that invaded day-to-day life, Hank and Marion had learned this truth throughout all the ups and downs of their own lives: when things seemed darkest, God was using these troubles to bring about His will; and along with it, tremendous peace and future blessings. Trusting God was where it all started.

CHAPTER 18

BUTTERFLIES AND
NEW BEGINNINGS

When Monday morning finally came, Cara could barely open her eyes. She remembered it was Monday, the first day of school, but the funk in her brain was relentless. Getting dressed was slow and difficult. She had no interest in eating breakfast and just picked at her cereal. Well, she thought, heaven forbid she should spill anything on her uniform! Plus, her stomach was ready to expel anything it encountered.

No one seemed to notice she was having trouble; they all had their own issues, and everyone was a bit cranky. Only her dad seemed cheerful, but even he was off in his own thoughts.

After inspection from the mother, the family got into the van. Cara was leaving the domain that had become her only shelter in a storm, as dysfunctional as it often was. Showing her typical aloofness under trying conditions, she sat in the back seat, not really looking at anything, her stomach in an uproar. How would she ever survive the dreaded first day of school? At least she didn't have to worry about throwing-up – her stomach was empty! A very good reason for not eating breakfast.

Upon arrival, the mother took the two little boys with her to an area called Pre-School. Dad, who had followed in his car, took Katie and Cara to an area called Intermediate Department, and Katie left them for parts unknown. Cara was grateful when her dad took her hand, softly speaking reassurances, picking up on her nervous demeanor. "You'll be okay. You have a very nice teacher. Don't worry."

Right. Nothing to worry about, Cara said to herself. She had trouble believing that.

Reaching her classroom, she gingerly peered in; the teacher was the only one in sight. "Why, Pastor Dan! I didn't expect to see you here!" the lady said, obviously surprised. "Are you staying awhile? I can put you to work, even though it is just the first day."

Then she noticed Cara, trying desperately to hide behind her father. "Is this Cara? Hello. Come on in; I'll show you where to put your things and where your desk is. Come on, it's okay."

Her father gave her a gentle push, and Cara left the citadel of protection he had been providing; gingerly, she advanced into this alien territory. The sign above the front board said, Mrs. Clark's Room: Home of the Monkeys– We Go Bananas for Jesus. At this Cara smiled. They knew Jesus here. Maybe it would be okay.

After a few brief moments of quiet conversation with the teacher, Pastor Dan, as Cara was to call him at school, left; he actually blew her a kiss before leaving, and he reminded her to go to the pick-up line after school; he'd pick her up there. At this point, all Cara could do was trust, not an easy thing after all she had been through.

Shortly the room was filled with noisy students. She sat up straight in her chair, looking at the front board, trying to be unnoticed; in truth, she felt like there was an earthquake inside her about to erupt. She was surprised when a boy brushed her shoulder as he walked by. He said, "You're new, aren't you? I'm Sammy. I sit over there," he said as he pointed to a chair up front. "I always sit in the front."

"That's because you're such a pain, Sammy!" a girl in the back shouted out. "Look! There's your picture on the front poster. You're the monkey in the front!" And at this, everyone laughed, all except for Cara and Sammy. Cara recognized the girl; it was Aubrie, one of the girls who had pushed her down yesterday at the park. Just that quickly, the teacher was standing next to the girl, quietly reprimanding her.

"I apologize, Sammy," she said. Then, after the teacher had moved on to other things, she went up to him and said, "I was wrong! You're the monkey in the back! Nobody would put your face up front!" And then she laughed as if she had come up with the best joke ever. Cara knew she needed to keep away from her. If at all possible.

A bell rang from somewhere, signaling the start of class. At their desks, everyone stood to recite the Pledge of Allegiance. Next, a devotion was read by Mrs. Clark; then, one of the students offered a prayer. This school might be okay, Cara thought to herself; apparently they were Christian, just like she was.

Cara knew, however, that kids are basically the same everywhere: some you could trust, but others, not. And you have to find out fast who's who.

In assigning a classroom friend for Cara, Britney volunteered before the teacher could say anything. This brought another wave of terror to Cara. If Britney was supposed to help her maneuver through the day, things could get really nasty! Fortunately, the teacher had someone else in mind, a girl named Sara, who seemed very friendly. Mrs. Clark was very aware of Britney's reputation; and while she was hopeful that Britney was making efforts in a positive direction, she was not willing to chance it on Cara's behalf.

As the morning got underway, Sara was very helpful in providing the guidance Cara needed–which book to get, where to put things, which class was next, etc. However, it was all too overwhelming for

Cara, just so much all at once; by the afternoon, she was exhausted. And Sara, as helpful as she had been earlier, had deserted her. Apparently, Cara was on her own.

It was just one o'clock, and the class had come in from lunch and recess; Cara took her seat, checked the schedule, and got ready for a lesson with the Spanish teacher who had just arrived. The lady had a very soothing voice as she spoke in her native tongue, asking questions to which the students gave rote responses, having already had three years of the class.

Unfortunately, Cara hadn't. First of all, she knew no Spanish; secondly, already spent from the overload of everything new, her head started bobbing, heavy eyelids began to droop, and drool commenced sliding down her chin. When the teacher gently touched her on the back, quietly saying her name, Cara was so startled, she jumped! For an instant she didn't know where she was. The ensuing laughter of her classmates brought her back to reality. Her face turned red, and the tears welling in her eyes were hard to force back into hiding. How could she ever live this down?

"Cara! Adonde es?" No response. "Do you speak Spanish?" the teacher asked.

"No." Cara's reply was soft and barely heard.

"Then you must stay awake and learn." And the teacher began again.

The afternoon couldn't go fast enough after that embarrassment, and when the final bell rang, Cara tried to exit the room quickly. It was then that Britney showed up. She stopped Cara and patted her on the back. "Good job, Cara! You only fell asleep once! See ya tomorrow!" Then she ran down the hall with her two friends, occasionally looking back at Cara and laughing.

Others who passed Cara in the hallway giggled as they went by. Once outside, she got in the pick-up line with Katie who had a little brother in each hand.

Looking at Cara's back, Jacob asked, "Why do you have that paper taped to your back?"

Katie took a look. "Really?!" laughed Katie. "Did you fall asleep in class today?" She removed the note and handed it to Cara. The words "I'm Sleepy" were printed in big letters.

So, that's why everyone was laughing at her. Cara's insides felt as though they would erupt at any minute. She took the paper. Drawing on years of building her outer armor of defense, her face took on the iron mask she had learned to wear. She stared straight ahead, emotionless, once more becoming stuck in the morbidity of her life.

Katie was the first to see their van in the car line. When it stopped, she mustered both brothers into their seats, and then sat on the front seat next to her dad. Slowly, Cara climbed over everyone to the seat in the very back.

"How was the first day?" Dad asked.

"It was school!" Katie was the first to speak, then added in her most sarcastic voice, "What do you think it was like, *Cara*?"

Picking up on his daughter's manner, he asked, "Cara, did something happen?" He was hopeful that Cara would have a good report.

Instead, she maintained her rigid look, staring out the window. She was thankful when Katie did not divulge the shame she had experienced.

Dad decided to let it go for the time being. Obviously it wasn't good, and he didn't intend to give Katie a chance to twist the knife any further. He knew he needed to speak with Katie about the treatment she was giving her sister. It was time for her to change her attitude.

Throughout the rest of the ride home and well into the evening, Cara maintained her silence. While a large part of her wanted to go to her hiding place, she instead chose to do her chores and get upstairs before anyone else. She was exhausted, embarrassed, and felt terribly alone. It was all she could do to get cleaned up, change into her pajamas, and crawl into bed.

As she lay there, she reflected that her life was on a continuous downward path that started with her mother's death. Desperately holding back the tears, she prayed, "Lord, why am I here? Nobody loves me. Are you even here, or have you left me, too?" She lay in the silence for what seemed forever; eventually she tucked herself in as deeply as she could. Exhausted from the day, sleep finally came, and with it some relief.

CHAPTER 19

THE MATH TUTOR

The school year had begun in earnest, and Cara's days became laden with the burdensome toil of the daily workload. She was far behind in just about every subject. And she knew it. Her classmates picked up on her slowness, and while some, like Jenna, tried to be helpful–"Mrs. Clark, can I help Cara?"–overall, her brain had checked out. Like Tom Sawyer, school became odious to her, and home life was no more a safe haven for her than Tom's had been for him.

While most classes were problematic, there were a few classes in which she drew comfort. In religion, which was the first class of the day, she was a shining star. She looked forward to it, finding the words of scripture they had to memorize to be reassuring; they grounded her in a way nothing else could. Her hand was extended in response to every question Mrs. Clark asked, and often her responses showed a maturity her classmates lacked. Unfortunately, this became a source of teasing by some of them, with Britney and her sidekicks leading the charge.

"Oh, Cara, did you get any special messages today?" Britney would sneak up on her in the hallway, and then she and her two friends would laugh and point at her, doing their best to belittle and hurt Cara. It wasn't long before Cara stopped raising her hand in any class. Even in reading, another class she found to be easy, her grades began to drop. Cara had no idea why those three girls treated her with such contempt. Unfortunately, she was letting them get to her, along with everything else. The downward spiral of her life seemed to be gaining momentum, her stoicism helping to dig the hole deeper.

Other classes were also difficult for Cara. She was behind in math, never having learned the basics; and history, science, and Spanish made no sense to her whatsoever – they *all* might as well be foreign languages! Another problem showed up with lunch: while she had always eaten the cafeteria lunches at her old school, here the mother insisted they make-and-take their own lunches from home. Unfortunately, Cara often forgot to take hers along in the morning rush, and she just went hungry. That made the afternoon lessons that much harder as she was unable to concentrate on an empty stomach. When the teacher sent a note home about the matter, Cara was scolded for her forgetfulness and for making the mother look bad.

No one seemed to take her side, to understand how difficult the transition was for her. Day by day, her life took on a crushing barrage of hardships, the hole getting deeper and deeper, and there seemed to be no end to it. If experiencing her mother's death was hard, this sequel was even more unbearable. She was failing life, and life was failing her.

By mid-September, almost four weeks into the year, a conference was requested by her teacher. Cara shuddered as she handed the note to her father. As much as she tried to maintain her unresponsive demeanor, her face fell, tears began to stream down her cheeks, and her shame became a salient signal that her life was a failure.

It fell to the dad to attend the appointment, the mother reminding him that Cara was his responsibility. Almost begrudgingly he accepted the request, not because he didn't want to go, but because, inwardly, he desired that his wife would enfold Cara as a member of the family. She would not, and there was little Dan could do to change it. Tuesday after school, the third week in September, Dan met with Mrs. Clark while Cara sat outside the classroom door, an offender not allowed to attend her own inquisition.

Shortly, and to her surprise, she was invited to join them. Now what? Her face was set in stone, but the contents of her stomach were about to make an appearance–she *had* to keep it all together!

"Cara," the teacher began, "it seems that school is really hard for you, and I'm very concerned about what I can do to help you. Can you tell me what your day is like? How you feel about being here, for example."

This surprised Cara. No teacher had ever asked her this. No one seemed to care what was happening to her. They mainly just found fault in her work. She hesitated; should she tell the truth, or just say nothing?

"Cara." Her dad spoke softly, kindly. "We're not here to make things harder. Mrs. Clark and I want to understand how we can help you. But we need you to tell us how."

Cara's big eyes glanced back and forth from one person to the other. Should she trust them with her feelings, including her inability to take it when others made fun of her, or should she protect herself from looking like a failure *and* a cry-baby?

Before she responded, Mrs. Clark took ahold of her hands and looked imploringly into her eyes. "Your life has been so hard. I don't know how you've been able to keep it all together." There was a pause; then Mrs. Clark continued, "It had to be very difficult to lose your mom, and I'm sure you're still trying to get used to all the changes since then. I have a feeling you missed a lot of school these last years just to stay home and help take care of your mom. Does that make sense to you? I'm sure she depended on you, and you did your very best to be there for her."

As much as she tried to hold it in, tears began streaking down Cara's cheeks. Why did they have to bring this up? Yes, her mom depended on her. Had she done her very best? Her mom was dead, so in Cara's mind, she had failed. Finally, without looking up, she nodded. All she really wanted to do at this point was get up and run away. She knew she had no hope of that. These two adults seemed intent on making her face her demons. Dear Jesus, she silently prayed, help me.

"School has always been hard for me," she began. "But this school is even harder. I can't do anything right! I'm so stupid!" Huge sobs began to cause her whole being to convulse, and try as she might, she could do nothing to stop them. Her dad reached over and put his arm gently around her, carefully drawing her in, desperately working to keep his own eyes from watering.

Mrs. Clark gave them both tissues. Then, in loving tones, she reminded Cara that just as her earthly father had his arms around her, her heavenly Father was doing the same. And, with Him, they would sort their way through all this. He had the answers, and He would provide the way. "Let's get down to the business of finding out what that is, shall we?"

It took a while for Cara's sobs to subside. The three of them prayed together, asking for direction, and very soon a plan was laid out. While Cara had fallen behind in reading, it was still something she could take care of on her own. Instead of using it as her escape, however, she had to do the work that came along with the reading assignment. Books she could read as a reward when her school work was finished.

There were, however, two things that, with immediate attention, Cara's day would be more productive: math and organization. First of all, to put things in order, Cara was shown how to fill out an assignment book. Each day's work was to be carefully recorded, subject-by-subject. Any long-range work would be written at the bottom of each page as a reminder to work on it until it was due. This was to be her daily work schedule.

"Is there someone in class who could help you with this, make sure you have all your assignments correctly recorded?" Mrs. Clark inquired. "What about Sara? I know she didn't follow through before, but she really likes to be helpful. Let's both of us talk with her tomorrow, see if she's willing. Okay?" Cara nodded her head in agreement.

It was evident by Cara's reaction that she was already feeling more confident. She was looking them in the eye instead of staring at the floor, and her overall posture was an encouragement. Maybe this plan was coming together, her teacher thought. She decided to forge ahead and look at another major concern.

Math was lurking in the darkness. Mrs. Clark brought it up, seeking how to get this mystery under control. She believed Cara's best chance was to work with a tutor. While her Dad was willing to help, he wasn't sure he would be that dependable – his work load as pastor was unpredictable, and usually very time-consuming. Someone else, after school or at home, was needed. The mother? No, she had her own work to do as well take care of the whole family. Plus, Cara thought to herself, the mother would not be willing to help her.

Would there be a teacher or upper grade student who could help her? Maybe, but Cara would need someone constantly until she was caught up. "Maybe Katie," Mrs. Clark suggested. "She's a good student, especially in math; and, she certainly is available, right?" With that, in their minds, the matter was decided, the discussion over.

With the problems solved to everyone's satisfaction—well, *almost* everyone—the meeting ended. Cara and her dad made their way home, riding in silence for some time, each unsure of the other's thoughts. Cara was the first to speak: "Dad, do you think Katie will help me?" Then more silently, "We don't always get along."

Dad was quiet for a while, trying to decide how best to respond.

"Cara, this is going to take two things: a lot of prayer, and a lot of patience. For you *and* for Katie. I'll speak to her, tonight, after supper. It'll work. She is a good student, likes math, and I know she likes to show it off...this might be her chance to shine!"

It did take some convincing to get Katie to agree to be Cara's math tutor. Dad encouraged her to take the job by referring to her love of teaching and her expertise in math; he further commented that the improvement in Cara's math scores would be her victory as well as Cara's; and, covertly, he mentioned that maybe there would be some cash remuneration! With that, Katie took the job, and she and Cara established a nightly routine of math help. It took a few rounds before the two of them settled on a plan:

> 1. Cara was to get started on the work at school and not wait until she got home.

> 2. Whenever possible, the teacher would be engaged in assisting Cara by grading that work immediately, thereby alerting them both concerning Cara's issues. Then, Katie would work on them at home.

It didn't take long for Katie to discover Cara's main problem: she did not have her number facts memorized. To solve this, Katie delighted in creating flash cards of the mysterious items that Cara's brain had not captured. It took repeated practice, but Cara's progress became a boon to their tenuous friendship; and, slowly, her math also improved. School was becoming more do-able, and the tension between the two of them began to ease. By the end of the first quarter, all Cara's grades had reached "C" level or better.

Then, the next monster showed up.

CHAPTER 20

CARA'S MISUNDERSTANDING

For Cara, day-to-day life was still somewhat tenuous. The second quarter was well under way, and with it the work load had increased. While she didn't need Katie's help every day, math was often a mystery she couldn't unravel. Fortunately, Katie was still willing to help, especially when her dad was willing to reimburse her for her time. With the improvement in Cara's organization, other areas of subject matter were at least being completed on time, and that alone helped Cara's sense-of-self improve greatly. She became more willing to be open to new friendships, and many of her classmates responded in turn.

Unfortunately, other things about the classroom were still causing anxiety. Cara had become the target of a series of covert messages, left in her desk, obviously aimed at bringing her down. She knew–or at least suspected–who the guilty parties were: Britney, Aubrie and Caroline, her three nemeses. It was hard to comprehend why these three girls were so full of animosity for her, but Cara decided to ignore their affronts and concentrate on the ones who wanted to befriend her. This wasn't easy. The three seemed to know just when Cara was most vulnerable, going out of their way to strike a blow. This made her an easy target when she least expected it. Unwittingly, Cara was about to set herself up for serious abuse.

It was the beginning of November, and more somber feelings of homesickness had taken over. Cara thought about her gramma putting out her fall decorations, trying her best to encourage everyone to celebrate the season, even though the Florida weather still felt like summer. She'd make pumpkin bread, pumpkin cookies, and anything else pumpkin she could find. Cara's mom would string fall leaves around their front door, and a big plastic pumpkin would be left on the porch. Best of all, they'd start planning Thanksgiving dinner; nothing much changed from year-to-year, but they each presented new recipes, just to see where the wind lay.

Sadly, her new family seemed too busy to consider a holiday still four weeks off. As much as she wanted to bring it up, Cara knew not to. Instead, she went to her secret place, looking over the happy playground scene. Why couldn't she put up fall decorations here? Finding some orange construction paper, she made her own pumpkin head, putting a big smile on its face. A scarecrow was added to the playground, and she made large black crows circling in the sky.

While this added some satisfaction, Cara wanted to do more, something that everyone could see and enjoy. Then she came up with an idea: school! The classroom! Maybe the teacher would be amenable to some decorations there, and Cara knew just what they could do. Everyone could make part of a paper chain out of construction paper leaves. They could be stapled together and then be hung on the walls. Her classmates could write Bible passages, poems, prayers, or just little notes about Thanksgiving on their leaves.

Unfortunately, what Cara didn't know was that the school had a yearly contest to see whose room would be decorated the best for the holiday. To this end, Mrs. Clark had already assigned several students to come up with ideas to decorate the walls, bulletin boards, and the inside of the classroom door. With Cara's plan, a train wreck was about to happen.

It was the first day of the first full week of November, a Monday, and Cara entered the room with her ideas, bolstered by her new-found sense of self. The bell rang, the class settled in, and Mrs. Clark was about to begin the devotion. Cara's hand went up. This wasn't unusual for Cara, but not first thing in the morning, before the devotion. Obviously, she had something important to say.

"Cara," said Mrs. Clark, "can it wait?"

Cara wasn't thinking. "Oh! I just have an idea, and I want to share it."

Mrs. Clark thought it might be a devotional thought, something appropriate to start the day. "Okay, Cara, what is it?"

"I think we should decorate the room for Thanksgiving, and I know what we can do. We can all be part of it!" Cara was so proud of herself for her boldness, she beamed from ear-to-ear. Then the bottom fell out. The gasps of her classmates soon turned to giggles.

Mrs. Clark was nonplussed! Cara's innocence was to be her downfall, again. After all the strides she had been making... Even Mrs. Clark was caught off guard as to how to stem the ensuing tragedy. "Cara," she finally said, "let's talk about this later. I think there are several ideas floating around, and we'll be glad to add yours to the mix." After getting the class under control, she continued with the day's devotion, Treasured by God. Cara's ears were deep red from embarrassment, and she didn't hear it at all.

Afterward, classes continued in the usual fashion: religion, math, English, reading, and social studies. All before lunch. Mondays were always loaded this way. Cara was thankful for the diversion of class work, but her insides roiled from her carelessness. How could she be so rash? What was she thinking?

While several classmates gave encouragement, Cara could feel the searing looks of her three antagonists, and she knew they would find a way to make her suffer for her blunder. All Cara wanted at this point was to stay under the radar.

Lunch came and went. Nothing. So far, so good. Cara decided that maybe she wrong. Maybe she could make it through the day without being accosted. However, Mrs. Clark still hadn't taken time to talk with her, and that bothered her even more. Maybe Mrs. Clark was too embarrassed, thought Cara. Maybe she had really caused a problem this time, and her teacher was angry at her.

When everyone was finally settled in their seats, Mrs. Clark announced that Spanish had been cancelled, and it was time to start the plans for their classroom decorations for Thanksgiving. She discussed the award by the student council for the best display, and then she let her appointed committee explain this year's theme and projects. While they were talking, she secretly approached Cara, hoping to assuage the girl's humiliation from her earlier gaff.

"Cara, what was your idea? I'd really like to hear it."

"Oh, it's nothing. Just something I thought of last night. I didn't know there was a committee and a contest. I'm sorry."

"It's okay, Cara. Maybe it can be added to the mix. Don't give up."

Then, Mrs. Clark was sidetracked by the chairperson of the decorations committee, and that conversation took precedence over Cara's awkwardness. They were making their assignments, and they were having trouble getting the cooperation needed for their projects. Mrs. Clark took control, and the committee brought out the items needed to complete the various ideas.

Cara, still lost in her embarrassment, never heard her name when it was called, and she wasn't aware of the group she was assigned to help; so she sat quietly, head down, trying to be invisible. After a while, noticing others standing in groups, she decided to walk around the room, trying to fit in somewhere. No one made any effort to include her; and, Mrs. Clark was busy keeping some boys on task, so she was no help to Cara either. She went to her desk and got out a book, pretending to read. Anything to look busy.

She was unable to concentrate. There was a lot of commotion in the room as the class got involved in their projects, and Cara felt more and more left out. Before long, however, she found herself getting bored. Then it came to her: her project was worth doing. She just had to get it started. Spying construction paper on the supplies table, Cara began to organize the way in which she would accomplish her vision. She could cut out leaf patterns and invite students individually to make their own. Each person was to create something on the paper: add glitter, stickers, color, lines. She would gather the leaves and make them into a chain by stapling them all together. She didn't consider where she would hang the completed project…that would come later. Right now, she had work to do.

As she was busy creating the leaves, Cara heard her name being called. "Cara! Get over here! You're on our committee." Dutifully, she joined the group, not entirely sure what was expected of her. In her group were three girls and two boys. Cara made six. In truth, the three girls did everything and complained when the boys goofed off. What they needed was someone to clean up the mess, and since Mrs. Clark had told them to include Cara, that would satisfy both needs.

This was not exactly what Cara had in mind. She wasn't just an after-thought, an add-on. Her project, on the other hand, was important, and it didn't take long for Cara to slip away and get back to it. Secretly, she engaged a few classmates at a time with instructions to complete a leaf using the supplies she had appropriated. Some students saw her request to be annoying, while others seemed glad for the chance to actually be artistic and contribute to the cause.

By the end of the day, Cara had collected 14 leaves, each one carefully produced. Tomorrow she would get each classmate to do at least 2 more. She would have new suggestions as to what a leaf could contain. When finished, there would be a very long chain! Then, where to hang it? She had some ideas about that, too.

The school day over, Cara made her way to the pick-up line.

Determined to keep what had happened at devotion time a secret, she put on her serious face and stood in line, waiting for dad to pick them up. Katie was not going to make fun of her today, she decided. She had her homework with her, so there would be no accusations there. That night, Cara finished all her work on her own, something that was happening more often than not lately.

At the supper table, the talk turned to the classroom decorations contest. Cara kept silent while Katie excitedly began to describe the ideas for her class's projects, especially since most of them were hers. Well, she *was* head of the decorating committee, as usual, and she expected to win the prize. Half way in, she stopped short, remembering that Cara's class would be in competition; then, she warned her—no, threatened her—not to tell, and not to copy her ideas! Cara smiled, promised she wouldn't, and that ended the conversation. No one suspected that Cara was a gifted artist and that she had her own story to tell. Now, if only she could figure out how to get it all done.

CHAPTER 21

COMPLETING THE PLAN

Tuesday, and classes began as usual. Decorating was assigned to the final period of the day, and parts of it would have to be finished at home, per Mrs. Clark's directions. Somehow it all had to be completed and put up by the end of the day Thursday as the judges would be making the rounds Friday morning to determine the winning class.

The day went slowly. The clock seemed to enjoy a more leisurely pace with everyone's eyes affixed to its hands. When the time for working finally arrived, it was as if a balloon filled with confetti had burst open, the students hurriedly forming into groups and organizing work details. Cara as well joined her group, seeing what she could do to help. Surely she would be needed, knowing the time was short.

Once again the three girls took charge, rather oblivious to their other three members. The boys began their usual distracting behavior, and Cara, totally unnoticed, decided she had more important work. Carefully she slipped away to work on her chain. It, too, needed to be done and added to the room's décor by the end of the day Thursday.

Checking her surroundings, she moved her work-station to the reading corner, assuming that no one would be using it this week. It was situated so that Mrs. Clark could keep an eye on it from her desk, but it was somewhat shielded from the rest of the class. This way it provided a hide-away for Cara and her clandestine plan. She acquired some more paper, cut out different leaf patterns, and then began looking for her targets, those students unengaged in everything but what they were supposed to be doing.

Some of the students actually questioned Cara. "What are you doing? What's this for?"

"It's something special for Mrs. Clark," Cara would respond with all seriousness. "She wants everyone involved with the decorations, so I thought we could each write stuff about Thanksgiving on paper leaves. You can do more than one. You can write a prayer, a poem, something you're thankful for, a Bible passage, even draw a picture if you want. It just has to be about Thanksgiving. That's all. You can bring them to me when you're done. I'm over in the reading corner."

With that, the project took on some authority. No one on her committee seemed to concern themselves about what Cara was doing, and Mrs. Clark secretly watched as her new shining star directed her project. It was Cara's idea, and as long as she handled it well, Cara would be given the needed latitude to complete it.

Wednesday afternoon, and decorating activities took a different turn. Since about half the class was more involved in distraction activities, the committee heads would be given time to work separately. That was fine with them. Of course, anyone who was interested and cooperative could join them – the girls would choose who that would be. The boys, so immature were obviously excluded; this way, the projects would certainly get done on time, and to perfection! To Cara, this meant she could work on her project, also. It, too, had to be finished and hung up on time.

Carefully, Cara made her way around the class, again inviting her classmates to decorate another paper leaf. This time no one asked what she was doing; it was for a special surprise.

Mrs. Clark continued to silently observe Cara's actions, wondering how her project would turn out.

For Cara, the hard part came next: making the chain and keeping it hidden. Borrowing the stapler from Mrs. Clark, she gathered all the leaves and went to the reading corner. One-by-one, she stapled them together, mixing up the colors and contents, hopefully making the finished product more interesting. Before long, there was a mound of paper leaves, almost 30 feet long when measured. Cara was ecstatic! Now, where to hang it all? That would involve a discussion with the teacher which meant revealing her activity of the past few days.

When Cara explained the project, Mrs. Clark gave no admonishment to Cara's methods. Instead, she turned the question back on her. "Where do you want to hang it?"

Every place Cara thought of was already taken. Even the ceiling was claimed by one of the groups. Maybe the door, Cara thought. No, the inside had also been assigned. On one of the white boards? No, those were needed for class. In the next moment of silence, Cara presented a viable idea. "Is anyone decorating the *outside* of the door?"

After some consideration, Mrs. Clark decided that would work. No class had ever decorated that area; it would be unique! She would provide the proper tape, and Cara could involve some classmates to help her. So excited, Cara gave her a sudden hug. Mrs. Clark felt a surge of delight, seeing how a tragedy from Monday was now turning into a positive affirmation of Cara's growth. Plus, she was seeing a side of Cara she hadn't seen before. This loving child's creativity, organization, and ability to involve her classmates was exceptional!

Suddenly the day was over, and the teacher watched as her students scrambled to put some order back into the classroom, grabbing their books and assignments to finish at home. Cara's smile as she left the room added a sense of fulfilment – she was finally finding a home. Mrs. Clark enjoyed the peace, hoping it would last, that the attacks from the three girls had ended. Maybe her prayers had been answered; maybe their hearts were turned, their darkness put away.

CHAPTER 22

THE AWARDS

Thursday afternoon was chaotic from one room to the next as the various classes set about the task of decorating. Each thought theirs was the best, sure to win the prize: an ice cream party after lunch on Friday.

Now, everyone in the room got busy. No time to waste, and no one was allowed to play around. Cara involved some boys to help move the chain to the outside of the door and assist in hanging it. While classmates noticed the movement, they regarded it as part of the commotion and went on with their own projects.

It took a while for the chain to look attractive. The end product was a double cross that was positioned on the top half of the door with a large circle around it. By the time it was completed, work in the classroom was pretty much finalized as well. Cara felt very contented with the overall appearance; she especially liked the messages each leaf conveyed.

"This room looks marvelous!" Mrs. Clark's eyes beamed with delight. "Good job, everyone! And, be sure to check the outside of the door – it's been given special attention this year as well. Thank you Cara and class – you each have a part in it!"

The bell rang that ended the day, and students filled the hallway, everyone on their way home. There was a small traffic jam outside

Mrs. Clark's room as students and teachers took a moment to appreciate the decorated door. Cara left, her heart ready to explode in her chest. Things seemed to be turning for her, she thought; maybe everything would be all right.

At home that evening, Katie again focused on the fabulous job her class had done in decorating their room. She just knew it would win this year. Now that it was all complete, she began to elaborate on the items that had been purchased and incorporated with the work she had her classmates complete. The message was obvious, and everyone just knew it was great! Even the teacher said so.

Cara sat quietly through all Katie's bragging, and when Katie chided her, she just smiled and said nothing. She wasn't going to say anything she might regret tomorrow.

Friday morning a committee made up of student council members and people from the office staff travelled from room to room, making notations and giving points as they judged the completed decorations. From the look on their faces, Mrs. Clark's room garnered special interest, mainly as a result of the cross on the outside of the door. Some frowned, some inspected the chain more closely, and others only observed it from a distance. Watching all this take place, Cara's stomach lurched with a sense of uncertainty. What had she done? Was there a problem? Certainly, Mrs. Clark wouldn't have let her put the chain on the door if it would cause a problem!

Then, a note was passed to her from an unknown source in the room. It said, "You better not have ruined this for us!"

What? No! Her chain looked beautiful, didn't it? What was wrong? Cara's countenance fell, her stomach again in turmoil. What had she done, honestly? Her shoulders slumped, and Cara, seated at her desk, shut out everyone and everything, unaware of the events of the rest of the morning. As each subject came and went, Cara's mind returned to the safety of stoic oblivion, a place where everything was numb, where she would let nothing in that might hurt.

Shortly before lunch, the classes were interrupted over the loudspeakers. The results of the Thanksgiving Decorating Contest were completed, and this year two classes were to be awarded instead of one. The first one, "Most Unique and Attractive" went to the eighth grade room. Their Pilgrim People display was an artistic fete in itself, and everyone should make sure to check it out. Since the eighth grade classroom was next to the office, loud, raucous cheers could be heard in the background.

The announcement continued. "We felt a second award was required this year because of a very special display that promoted the real theme of Thanksgiving, that God is the giver of all our blessings. This new award, 'Best Class Involvement of the Theme', goes to fourth grade. Everyone in the class took part in producing the chain of leaves that decorates the outside of their classroom door. It is not only unique, but the messages are beautiful testaments to our wonderful heavenly Father. Take time to read them. Just don't be late for class..." Again, you could hear the hooting of the eighth grade next door to the office. Cara's room also erupted with loud cheers, and Cara, rousing slowly out of her detachment, received many unexpected accolades from her classmates. Mrs. Clark couldn't help but beam. Things were changing for the better, for Cara. She was sure of it.

The bell rang for lunch, and after saying their prayer, Mrs. Clark led the class out to the picnic tables for lunch...and, ice cream to follow. What she didn't notice were the three girls who stayed behind, up to some mischief; soon, they joined the class, unnoticed by all but a few other girls. "What were you doing?" one of them asked.

"None of your business!" was the response. And everyone in hearing distance knew to keep it to themselves as well. These girls were not trustworthy girls, and no one wanted to be on the receiving end of what they could dish out.

Too soon lunch was over, and school was back in session. The Spanish teacher was actually given time that afternoon for class, although what to expect after the lunch award, she could only guess. She doubted it would be productive, so she planned a movie, a familiar cartoon in Spanish, trying to quell a possible riot. Outside her purview, three girls were candidly watching Cara, waiting for her to open her desk. It didn't happen – no materials were needed, so the lid was never raised.

Mrs. Clark returned for the last period of the day, forty minutes of trying to keep-the-lid-on as she remarked to a colleague earlier. She decided to use the time to visit with the class about the events of the week – the decorating, group work, the final award: what went well, what needed improvement, and, especially, how did they feel about their special award? The burning question from one girl was why Cara had been given special permission to do her own project. Others voiced the same concern. Some in the class just groaned. Because of Cara, they all got ice cream. "What's so bad about that?" several of them proffered.

"All right. I admit, I let Cara do her project; but how many of you have a leaf on the door? She wasn't the only one who worked on it. And several of you helped her put it up. So, it wasn't just Cara's project. It's probably the only thing in the room everyone had a part in. So many of your messages are right from your hearts. I personally loved them. We can all feel good about everything that was accomplished this week. And, there was ice cream, right?"

Nervously, Cara had opened her desk…only slightly. She didn't like being the center of any discussion and wanted to hide behind the lid. She could feel eyes glaring at her; she didn't know why. Then she discovered the item: a piece of paper with a drawing of a disfigured face, the name "Cara" written above it. Around the outside were the words, "Stupid", "Creep", "Ugly". Notes at the bottom said, "Too bad you didn't die with your Momma" and "Go home! Nobody wants you here!"

Softly she closed the top of her desk. Her countenance fell, her outward appearance not betraying what she felt. She hoped no one noticed that she had read their hateful note. She wasn't entirely sure who had done this, but she was pretty sure it was Britney and her two friends. Why did they treat her this way? What had she done to them?

The day finally came to a close, and Mrs. Clark dismissed the class. Cara left quietly, got into the car pick-up line, and climbed to the back seat when her dad arrived. "How was the day? Hey, who won the decorating award?"

"Yeah, Cara, whose idea was it to put the paper leaf chain on the door? Don't you know that's saved for a Christmas decoration? Your class shouldn't have won ice cream for it. That was cheating!"

Cara gave no response. Instead, she looked out the side window of the van. How could such an exciting day turn so ugly, she wondered? Why did her sister berate her like this? Why couldn't her classmates just accept her? What would it take?

Dad felt the icy undercurrents of some problem. Cara's face seemed contorted, eyes focused out the window; she said nothing verbally, yet her demeanor relayed that demons were again attacking in full gear. He felt unable to draw her out of her angst. As soon as they arrived home, Cara's fleeting steps took her to her private place; she needed a safe haven, away from the horrors that were again taking over her life.

The rest of the weekend, she went about taking care of her usual business, spending time in her hiding place as much as possible. There was no way she could face a confrontation from anyone. Monday would come soon enough. She had to formulate a plan by then, some way to fend off the terrors that were rising against her.

CHAPTER 23

MUDDLING THROUGH

Saturday, and the usual housecleaning jobs were first on the list. Maybe, the mother said, if there was time later in the day, they could go look at the fall displays in the various stores.

Mother was actually the first to say something about Cara's demeanor. "What's going on with Cara?" she asked Katie, as if she would know.

"No idea. She came home from school like this yesterday. Hasn't said a word. You want me to get her?"

"No, your father can deal with her. After all, she's his responsibility." And the two of them shared their private smile. "I'll tell you what. Sammy and Jacob want to go outside to play. They like Cara, and she's actually pretty good with them. Maybe they can get her out of this sour mood."

Unenthusiastically, Cara took the boys out to the back yard. With all their toys to choose, they liked it best when Cara played with them. This lightened her day somewhat, and she began to play various styles of tag with them. It took about an hour before she was out of breath and looking for something else to do. She sat on the porch step, and both boys came and plopped themselves down on top of her lap, struggling to be the only one there. Arguing and pushing, each boy wanted to be Cara's special boy, her only boy.

Jacob, being older and stronger, pushed his brother off forcibly, and Samuel began to cry – more from hurt feelings than hurt body parts. Angry, hurtful words were slung back and forth.

"Stop this!" Cara said, louder than she meant to. Then, in a softer voice, "This isn't how you treat each other. You're brothers! Jesus wants you to love each other, not hurt each other. Now say you're sorry."

The boys looked sheepishly first at Cara, then at each other. Jacob was the first to offer his apology: "I'm sorry, Sammy."

Sammy looked at his older brother and smiled. "I'm sorry too, Jacob."

"Friends?" Cara asked, and then began to tickle each one. Soon they were laughing, and a new game of tag began. This was the best she had felt since yesterday. But with that thought, her sadness began to creep inside again.

"Oh, Jesus!' she thought. "What's going on? Why does it have to be so hard? Why am I here?"

From the back door, the mother called all three to come in for lunch. They were going to run errands this afternoon, she added, "So let's get a move on!"

It was noticeable that Cara's spirits were lifted, somewhat, and mom and Katie winked at each other. "Hey!" Jacob shouted. "Did you just wink?"

It was something he had just learned, and he was excited to practice the technique himself. Glancing from one person to another, he attempted it over and over, bringing down the house in giggles and laughter. That was all that was needed. Lunch was devoured, and they all worked together to clear off the table; then they piled into the van for errands and sight-seeing.

The afternoon proved to be a healing potion to Cara's disposition. After picking up needed groceries, they went on the promised spree to check out the neighborhood. In their subdivision, a number of houses competed for the most garish displays, and even in the daylight, the illumination and sound effects were phenomenal. Street after street produced more glitz and glamor than Cara had ever imagined possible. Even Jacob and Samuel, who usually took afternoon naps, were big-eyed and wide-awake as the displays passed by the window. If Cara was homesick for fall, this helped to satisfy her desire, and she began to get in the mood for Thanksgiving. That is, until she remembered the incident at school. By the time they arrived home, she was back in her depression. As the evening progressed, her moodiness was about to drown her.

"Something has to be done to help that girl," the mother commented to her husband when the supper dishes were cleared. Cara had disappeared to her secret place, although it wasn't so secret anymore, and dad went to the garage to see what the problem was.

"Cara? Are you here?" he asked as he approached the boxes that hid her private space. "Can I talk with you?"

Cara was slow to respond, hoping he would give up, which he didn't, and she was forced to make an appearance.

"Cara? What's going on? Mom says you've been in a bad mood all weekend. Is that true?" No response, her face and eyes focusing on the floor. "Cara, what happened? Please tell me. Please." Still nothing. "Cara, look at me. Please, look at me."

Cara's eyes fixed on his face, but her head never raised. She had to stay strong, she felt. To give in now would be defeat, and she would not – no, *could* not – give in. To do so was to submit to foolishness, to admit her faults, to confess that she was to blame. And if it came to that, how would she ever be able to live with herself? Life was hard enough. If she could just get through this, she thought. What did this man want with her? Who was he? Why couldn't he just leave her alone, leave her with her grandparents, leave her to, she didn't know what.

"Cara," he began, "I can't imagine what it's been like for you, to lose your mother and then be thrust into this family, people you never met. We want so much for you to make your home here."

Cara's voice surprised them both. "Why? Nobody wants me here! Nobody likes me! The kids at school make fun of me; they write notes telling me they wish I had died with my real mom! Why? Why do I have to live here? It's not my home!"

"I thought the kids in your classroom liked you. Didn't they win a prize because of a great idea you had to decorate your classroom door? I heard you did a good job getting everyone involved." He paused but got no response. "Who's making fun of you; who wrote this note you're talking about?"

Again, silence. Then, "I don't want to talk about it. I'm not a 'tattle tale'." And with that, she turned away, went into the house, and went up to the bedroom. Dad knew the time would come for more talk. At least Cara had opened up about some of her dilemmas, and he felt encouraged that the necessary healings might finally start.

CHAPTER 24

CONFRONTATION

Monday morning, and Cara's insides were roiling with the turmoil that had encased her weekend. She had not slept well. At all! Furthermore, the talk with her father had opened up more than she wanted to divulge. She had spent Sunday night in a semi-conscious state, her mind continuing to bring up the events that ended the school day on Friday; Cara had no idea how she would face the people who had written that hateful note.

Katie's alarm rang, and she got out of bed, mindful of the disruptions Cara's tossing and turning had caused through most of the night. "Cara. Come on. Get up." Cara's stomach and head seemed to be controlled by circus clowns banging on large drums. She looked sick, and she felt worse. Maybe she could just stay home for the day.

"No such thing, not in this household," she was told. She didn't have a fever, so there was no reason to skip school.

"What's bothering you?" the mother asked at breakfast in a kinder voice that even surprised her.

"I just feel sick," was all Cara would say.

"Cara, I know something happened to you at school Friday. What was it?" Dad must have said something to the mother.

"Nothing. Nothing happened. I just feel sick." This mother was not her ally. She would confide nothing to her.

With that, the conversation ended, and Cara got her things together. Katie shrugged her shoulders when her mother's silent query sought her advice. Everyone got into the van, and Cara's long ride to school began, certain of an execution by her three rivals sometime during the day.

As usual, she was the first student in the fourth grade room since the mother, a teacher, had to be at school early. Mrs. Clark was there, expecting Cara; she gave her time to organize her materials before approaching her desk. Noticing Cara's demeanor, she moved closer to her.

"Cara." She spoke the name softly, standing right by her desk. "I know something happened Friday before you left school. And I looked in your desk and found this paper." Mrs. Clark had in her hand the paper Cara was trying to avoid. She was angry that the teacher had invaded her privacy, allowing this emotion to usurp her deeper feelings.

"You had no right to go into my desk!" Cara hastily responded, working hard to hold back her tears.

"Cara. I'm very angry at the people who wrote this and then had the nerve to leave it in your desk on Friday! It was very wrong of them to treat anyone this way!" Try as she might, Cara could not hold back the watershed that had been building since Friday. Gently putting her arm around Cara, Mrs. Clark continued, "This is not what Jesus wants his children to do. Cara, they are wrong! You are not the one in trouble. What they said is full of hatred, and they need to be held accountable. That's why I looked in your desk."

"If they find out you have the note, they'll think I tattled! Then everyone will make fun of me! No one likes a tattle-tale!" Cara's emotions were raw, and her sobs became great heaves that shook her body violently.

"Okay, Cara, but listen." Mrs. Clark spoke softer but with a firmness that was meant to convey the seriousness of her words. "When someone hurts another person, says the kind of things these three girls wrote to you, they are wrong; we cannot let that go. They have to own up to what they did and admit it was wrong; then, they can receive forgiveness. Jesus loves them, but they don't understand that, so they don't live like Jesus wants them to live. With Him, they can change. But they have to be held accountable for *this*!"

As students began entering the room, the conversation was put on hold. The look Mrs. Clark gave Cara was filled with love, and Cara turned her attention to getting ready for her first class, trying desperately to hide her red, swollen eyes. Somehow her classmates knew to leave her alone, and Cara sat with her head down, occasionally wiping her drippy nose with the back of her hand. She didn't know what the consequences of the conversation would be; she would have to trust someone, and her teacher, out of necessity, was the only one available at this moment.

CHAPTER 25

BUTTERFLIES AND BUMBLE BEES

Thanksgiving break was still two weeks away; the class was restless and talkative. Mrs. Clark had learned over the years to enjoy the atmosphere, knowing it just needed to be channeled. She walked around, greeting her fourth graders, making small talk about their weekend, surreptitiously leading up to the devotional thought she planned to use to start the day.

The bell rang, and the students gradually took their seats. It was time to begin. After brief comments about the decorations in the room, Mrs. Clark questioned the class about what we use to decorate our hearts, to show our faith. "I'm reading Philippians 2:1-5 – *If you have any encouragement from being united with Christ, if any comfort from his love, if any fellowship with the Spirit, if any tenderness and compassion, then make my joy complete by being like-minded, having the same love, being one in spirit and purpose. Do nothing out of selfish ambition or vain conceit,* (at this point, her eyes lit on each of the three problem children and continued reciting from memory, her words emphasized and clipped) *but in humility consider others better than yourselves. Each of you should look not only to your own interests, but also to the interests of others. Your attitude should be the same as that of Christ Jesus."*

With that, the reading ended, and the discussion centered on the last sentence. "What happens when someone doesn't have the attitude of Jesus?" Mrs. Clark continued. While some students looked aside, others raised their hands, some giving very pointed responses about punishment and teaching them a lesson.

"What's the lesson, and how do we help them learn it?" Mrs. Clark asked.

A boy in the back spoke out, "The lesson is that Jesus loves us, and that we should love each other, just the same way. And that's how people learn it."

Mrs. Clark nodded her head and looked around the room. "I like that," she commented. "Jesus loves us, and we love each other." The devotion ended with a prayer led by a student, and the day began. For the first time since she had left this room on Friday, Cara's spirit eased. However, there was a lot of Monday ahead of her, and the confrontation with the three girls was bound to happen, sometime during the day.

And it did…forcefully! After religion, students in grades 4 through 8 changed classes according to their level in math. Cara was in the remedial group which met in the classroom two doors down. As she made her way to the room, Britney came up from behind and forcefully shoved her into the wall, shielded by her two compatriots. "You better not have told! If you got us in trouble, you'll pay for it!"

Just that fast, Mrs. Clark was behind them, her voice quiet and forceful. "You three! To the office! Now!" Their eyes big, their demeanor showing fear, the three troublemakers quickly exited the area, Mrs. Clark close behind. Within minutes, one of the office workers was seen going into Mrs. Clark's room, an assignment in her hands. Cara was shaking. A classmate grabbed her arm and dragged her to her math room, explaining to the teacher why they were late.

"Now I'm really gonna get it!" Cara thought to herself. She had no idea how things worked at this school, but at her old school, you didn't trust the adults to do the right thing. She knew her trip to the office was not far away; she thought to herself, *"Those three girls will make up a story about me, and, with three against one, who will believe me?"* The call came shortly, and it seemed as if the butterflies in her stomach had turned to bumble bees, all stinging her at once.

What she hadn't counted on was Mrs. Clark, her dad, and that this wasn't her old school.

CHAPTER 26

THE SOLUTION

Two students accompanied Cara to the office. That's how it worked. Otherwise, Cara would have run out the door as fast as she could to who knew where – just out of here! She should have run away long ago. Why hadn't she? Oh, yeah. Nowhere to go. Nobody wanted her, she reminded herself. How could things get so ugly? Why had her life become so hard?

"Mom," she said to herself, "I'm sorry. It would be so much better if you hadn't died." The tears began to form in her eyes.

"NO!" she silently scolded herself. "Don't be such a baby!" She quickly wiped away the wetness, hoping her two escorts hadn't noticed. If they had, neither said anything and just deposited her with the secretary.

After a minute or so, Cara had a big surprise. Her dad came from the principal's office and took her by the hand to another room. He moved two chairs so they would face each other, and in this privacy, he took her hands in his; Cara was surprised when she looked in his face to see he was holding back his own tears.

"Oh, Cara," he began, "I had no idea what you've been going through. I knew some things were hard for you, but nothing like this. I'm so sorry for what's been happening."

He must have seen the note Britney and her friends had left in her desk, Cara thought. As much as she tried to hide her feelings, sitting as stiff as she could, tears began to trickle down her cheeks, betraying the little bit of self-esteem she was working to retain. Still, she said nothing in reply.

"Cara, you understand that what those three girls did was despicable. I don't know what made them act this way. They're bullies, Cara; and they will pay for what they did!"

"What do you mean, 'pay for what they did'? They're just stupid. That's all," she quietly muttered.

Cara's dad tried to explain that their behavior was full of meanness and hatred, and they had to be taught not to treat others that way ever again. There had to be consequences for them to learn this.

The room went silent; again, Dan continued trying to explain all this to Cara, but she interrupted him. "They act that way because they think nobody loves them. They don't know Jesus loves them, and they don't love Him back. They should, but they don't."

Dumbfounded, he had no words to respond to this. How could a 9-year old have such a deep understanding of human nature? He was truly speechless, and the silence between them equaled the distance in their relationship.

Just then, the door was carefully opened, and they were asked to join the others in the principal's office. The three girls were sitting in a corner, their faces downcast and streaked with tears, their eyes red. They were not willing to make eye-contact with Cara or her father. The principal spoke. "Cara, your classmates have something to say to you. Girls?"

"I'm sorry." Britney was the first to speak. The others nodded and added the same brief apology.

"That's it?" asked the principal. "What did we talk about? Didn't it mean anything to you?"

"Okay! I'm sorry I made fun of you! Can I go now?" Britney's apology was too full of anger to be regarded as serious.

"Why are you so mean to me? What did I do to…." Cara's question was interrupted.

"What did you do? You *came* here! That's what you did! You messed up my world. We were in charge before you came. But you were the *new* girl! Suddenly, everyone wanted to be your friend, do things your way. And you're such a 'do-gooder'. *You just love everyone!* Why did you have to come here?"

Mrs. Clark went over to Britney and started to take her hand; Britney pulled it away, trying to shield herself, and tightly folded her arms over her chest. Her two friends just stared at her, then at Mrs. Clark. What was going on? As usual, they took their cue from their friend and assumed the same posture, hoping to put on a united front that would protect them from the obvious dangers that were headed their way.

Mrs. Clark picked up the commentary. "Britney, Aubrie, and Caroline, I've spoken with each of you about this kind of behavior in the past. You've lost recesses; I've talked with your parents, and you've had to write letters of apology; and I also told you that if you didn't stop treating your classmates, especially Cara, this way, you would be suspended from school. Do you remember that?"

The girls looked at the floor.

Mr. Huntly, the principal, took over the discussion at this point. "I've called your parents, and you each will be picked up from school shortly. You are suspended for the next three days. Do you understand what this means? This is serious! Your behavior stops now, or we'll move on to the next punishment, which may mean you won't continue attending this school."

All three girls looked directly at the principal, mouths and eyes wide open, obviously in shock at his pronouncement.

"You mean we'll be *expelled*?" Aubrie's hushed tone spoke loudly. "My gramma's gonna kill me!"

Caroline sat with her eyes fixed on Mr. Huntly, the understanding of her errant behavior beginning to set in. "I won't be able to sit down for a week!" she said softly. "That's what my dad said the last time I got in trouble."

Through all of this, Cara kept her eyes fixed at a spot on the floor. While part of her was glad the three girls were being punished for the way they treated her, part of her also felt sorry for them. Why wouldn't they let Jesus love them? Why are they so stupid? She wanted to speak, but something inside wouldn't let her. Her dad's arm was around her shoulder, and she could feel his eyes watching her. What did he want? What was he thinking? Cara had no answers, but she sat still, frozen, giving no indication as to what was going on in her head.

Mrs. Clark excused herself from the room – there was a math lesson to teach – and indicated that Cara should go along with her. The other adults agreed. As they left the room, one of the parents arrived in the office; Cara was glad to leave this place and get back to class, even if was math. Her father stayed behind. As he looked Cara in the eyes, she saw a look she had never seen from him; something like love. She almost smiled back. Maybe her future was changing. Maybe.

CHAPTER 27

THE LESSON

The walk back to the classroom was silent, neither Cara nor Mrs. Clark saying anything, each seemingly lost in her own thoughts. Cara still felt bad for the three girls, but there was also relief that she wouldn't have to put up with the venom they spewed her way. The animosity she felt from several classmates had been orchestrated by the three; she had figured that out some time ago. Still, she couldn't understand why they so desperately wanted to hurt her. Her mother had explained it to her long ago when she had been bullied at her old school, but why did they feel unloved? Their mothers, or grandmother, were coming to pick them up, so they had someone who loved them, didn't they?

Reaching the classroom, Mrs. Clark stopped. "Cara," she said, "let's talk about this later. I know you've been the target of their actions, and I feel awful about how terrible it got."

Cara again fought back tears. She didn't blame Mrs. Clark. She didn't blame her classmates. If anyone, she blamed herself. Her guilt about her situation ran deep into her core being. As far as she was concerned, this was all about what she had done, or failed to do. Her mother's death was the salient proof of that, and it marked her for life. She strained to put on a solid outer look – she dared not show weakness – and she struggled to retrieve the stoic exterior that had become her stronghold, her only protection.

The two of them went inside. Math class had just ended, and the hallway was filled with students changing rooms for third period; they both took their respective places in the classroom and got ready for reading.

Cara could feel the eyes of her classmates following her to her desk; although no one spoke, they all wondered what had just transpired. No one knew. But they all surmised that it was something big; if not, where were Britney, Aubrie, and Caroline? Cara gave away nothing in her demeanor, nor did she look at anyone in particular. Reading class began as if everything was normal. But Cara's mind was still in another dimension; neither did Mrs. Clark betray anything in her voice or manner, and the lesson simply continued as usual.

From there on the progression of the daily routine was tenuous; everyone knew something was wrong and that it had to do with Cara. She didn't dare look around or make eye-contact with anyone. Even Mrs. Clark seemed to fumble her words occasionally. Mid-morning when science was supposed to begin, she put the lesson down and announced she had something that needed to be brought out into the open. If Cara had felt shaky before, her system went into overload now. Just keep it together, she told herself, her eyes focused on her lap.

"Something has been going on in this room that needs to stop." Cara sat at her desk, wishing she could just disappear. "Some of you have been involved – unfortunately – with class bullying. While it was led by three girls, I know more of you went along with it, maybe some of you not as much as others; that doesn't mean you are any less guilty. You'll find out sooner or later, so let me just inform everyone right now of the consequences of these actions. First of all, Britney, Aubrie, and Caroline have been suspended for three days." Gasps erupted around the class; some, however, produced wry smiles, proud they had not taken part in this behavior. Cara stubbornly held her ground.

Next, Mrs. Clark proceeded to alert the students to further repercussions if these actions repeated themselves in any way. One boy who had befriended Cara wanted to know why the three treated Cara the way they had – "Why were they so nasty to Cara?" he inquired.

"Good question," Mrs. Clark responded, and decided to open the discussion to the class.

At first, no one said anything, nor did the teacher offer any observation. She let the silence permeate the room. Would anyone dare to admit their own shortcomings? Being part of the bullying or failing to stand up to it was equally wrong, a sentiment that had been drilled into them often. To say anything now was to accept the accusation, and no one wanted to head down that trail. Interestingly, Cara was the one who finally broke the barrier.

"They don't know that God loves them," she said. The room stayed silent. "People who don't know they are loved try to hurt others. It's just their way of reaching out for help."

Still more silence. Finally, Mrs. Clark took up the baton. "Do you agree? Is that the reason for the bullying? What about those of you who went along with it, maybe even added to it? Is what Cara said true?"

From there the conversation started. Some agreed, others not; comments went both ways until Mrs. Clark brought up another concern. "What do we do about it? What do you think should be the consequences for this behavior, whatever the reason?"

Discussion went from one extreme to another, some calling for suspension for anyone involved, others taking the route of mercy, requiring the culprits to have to write a paper explaining their actions and promising not to do it again. Due to the lateness of the morning, the final decision was tabled. The class had to go to music, then lunch, and the afternoon was taken up with other daily requirements that prevented anything further.

"Let it sink in," thought Mrs. Clark. Teaching and learning don't always happen at the same time. And this was too important to rush.

CHAPTER 28

THE LEARNING CURVE

It was actually three days before Mrs. Clark opened the matter again. She wanted the matter to percolate before returning to the problem. Also, she purposely waited for the three absentees to be back in attendance, wanting to make sure they were included in any further conversations and, especially, decisions. Just because they had served three days of suspension didn't mean they were exempt. And they needed to know their classmates' opinions of their intolerable behavior. It was Thursday, and enough of an interval had elapsed to take up the discussion concerning handling bullying in the classroom.

This time it didn't take long for someone to break the ice. Punishments were suggested, the pendulum swinging both ways. "They shouldn't be allowed back in school" was on one side, and "They should write a paper and apologize" was on the other. Eventually a list was formed from the various ideas:

1. Loss of recesses for a week
2. Write a paper of apology to be read aloud to the whole class; Mrs. Clark would read it first to make sure it was acceptable

3. No privileges in the classroom for a week (like handing out papers, using the reading corner, being a helper, etc.)

4. Any further problems would restrict them from participating in any class projects for a month– such as decorating the room, birthday treats, etc.

"Is everyone satisfied? Does everyone agree to this?" Mrs. Clark addressed the class, wanting everyone to take ownership of the contract. With no further comments, she continued: "I think this is good. Now, someone needs to write this so we can all sign it. Like a poster, maybe. Caroline, you're a good artist. Would you do this for the class? Maybe you can get help from…someone." Looking up, Caroline nodded her agreement. It was a chance for her to be brought back into the fold, and she was actually thankful Mrs. Clark offered her the olive branch.

Unexpectedly, Cara raised her hand. "Mrs. Clark, I think there's something else we could do."

At this, there was a brief pause as well as a quizzical look from the teacher; however, since Cara had been the most recent target, Mrs. Clark was willing to allow some latitude.

"When people are bullies," Cara continued, "they have to know about love and forgiveness. Otherwise, they won't change. If we all write something about it, like a paper or a Bible passage, maybe that would help to get the point across."

There was a moment of silence, and then a brief nod of agreement from a few friends.

"I like your idea, Cara," the teacher commented. "Maybe that could be more voluntary, though. I think this has to come from a person's heart – it can't be forced. But we can invite anyone who would like to write something to do so. In fact, it could be extra credit for religion or English, just to encourage it." Some members of the class smiled and nodded agreement with this, always ready to respond to something if it meant getting extra credit. "Let's make this one due tomorrow, Friday. I know that's short notice, but I'd like to act on this right away so we can move on."

This was fine with Cara as she was already constructing her paper in her mind.

The rest of the day actually went much more smoothly. Mrs. Clark's main concern was for the three girls, that their behavior would change. For now, it seemed they were headed in the right direction, but the truth on the outside was not always the truth on the inside. Mrs. Clark wondered, however, if anyone would write the paper Cara had suggested. Besides Cara, that is. Somehow she knew Cara had something on her mind that still had to be said.

CHAPTER 29

THE BOILING POT

As school ended, Cara gathered her books together and headed for the door. "Thank you, Mrs. Clark," she added as she left the room.

Cara was already mentally organizing her paper and seemed oblivious to anyone in her vicinity. She made her way to the car line, almost floating on air. As she waited with Katie and the boys, Britney came up from behind and bumped her, almost pushing her into the line of traffic.

"Oh, I'm so sorry! Please *forgive* me!" No one could miss the sarcasm in Britney's voice. Cara stared in disbelief. She did not respond, however, which prompted her half-sister, Katie, to take special interest in what she had just witnessed. Katie waited, however, until they were all in the car and on the way home before she commented.

"So, Cara, what was that about?" she asked, her voice full of sarcasm.

Cara was silent, her eyes focused on whatever was outside the window. "What was 'what' about?" her dad innocently inquired.

Katie was unaware of her father's attendance at the meeting on Monday, and that he was instrumental in helping the school deal with the problem of bullying. She forged ahead in a sassy manner of speaking, thinking she was privy to inside information. "Oh, I hear there's been a problem with bullying in Cara's room. And I was just wondering why that girl purposely bumped you in the back, Cara…and you didn't say a word!" Her smile at her father was intended to influence his reaction. And it did. Just not what Katie expected.

"Katie?! What's this about?" His expression showed both surprise and anger. "Why are you speaking to Cara this way?" He paused, waiting for his daughter to respond. Instead, Katie's face took on a scowl, her mouth open in amazement.

"You need to apologize to your sister right now!" her father stated. When he got no response, he continued. "I won't allow you to treat her with such disrespect. I mean it! No more of this behavior."

"What did I do? Why are you yelling at me? She's the one you should be yelling at! She's the cause of all the problems in fourth grade!" Katie's sudden flare-up at him was not what Dad expected. It caught him off guard for a minute. Then, with her arms folded in front of her, she blasted him again! "And she's NOT my sister! She may be your daughter, but that doesn't make her my sister. Even Mom says so. You can just ask her!"

What? Dad couldn't believe what he had just heard. It took him a few minutes to calm himself. Was this true? Had his wife actually said that? If so, it explained a lot of things that had been going on over the last several months. He had tried to ignore the small incidents, the hushed comments between his wife and Katie, hoping he just needed to give them some space. He didn't want to believe his wife would be so callous toward a child who had just lost her mother, no matter what other considerations were in the mix.

Finally, he spoke. "Katie, I don't know what conversation has taken place between you and Mother. But your attitude and behavior toward Cara has to change. When we get home, I want you to go to your room and stay there. I'll speak with you later." By the tone in his voice, everyone knew not to push the discussion any further. Dad had reached a decision.

The car was silent for the rest of the trip – even the two little boys sat quietly. Katie, however, was fuming on the inside. When they finally arrived home, she stomped into the house and up the stairs to her room; she slammed the door, knowing that when Mom got there, she would have her ally, and Dad would have to back down. She knew she was right, and dad was wrong, and that's all that mattered.

Cara, on the other hand, was frightened by what had just transpired. She had been on the receiving end of Katie's anger in the past, but she didn't know Katie would speak to her dad this way. What was next? She focused on trying to be invisible. Sitting quietly in the back of the van and looking out the window, her goal was to avoid eye contact with anyone. She did not want to be part of the fallout of Katie's behavior. This outburst was not what she had expected, and so far beyond her comprehension. Her insides were again in turmoil.

Once home Cara made it her responsibility to attend to the two boys, getting them each a snack, and then took them to their play room. As soon as they were settled, she made a bee-line for her private space. She didn't want to deal with her sister, or her dad either, for that matter. Plus, she had a paper to write, and that was of most importance to her right now.

Out in the driveway, Dad sat behind the wheel of the car for several minutes instead of going right into the house; he was nonplused. What was going on with Katie? What had just happened between them? Could he have been so clueless of the animosity his wife had built up toward Cara? Had she really infected their daughter with loathing for her? He knew when he insisted that he bring Cara into the household there would be a time of adjustment, but he didn't expect the repercussions he had just witnessed. He also expected that his wife would be more accepting of this little child, of her plight in losing her mother. Besides being an early childhood teacher, she was a mother, and a Christian. Didn't that mean anything? Was she still holding on to her anger against him, taking it out on Cara? Furthermore, how long was she going to continue to hold on to it?

Finally, he went inside. He checked on the two boys, then went into the office, badly in need of some solitude to figure this out. Sitting there, he knew he needed to speak to Cara, to tell her that Katie was wrong, that his wife was wrong, that she *was* his daughter. But there was more.

How could he tell her the truth of who she was? What were the words he could use to explain what had happened over 9 years ago that created her life and made her part of him; how a late night in a pastor's office and the loneliness of two people lent itself to an indiscretion that resulted in the creation of this child? He knew his wife still held this against him, but it baffled him how she could she be so unfeeling, so hurtful to Cara. And what had happened that influenced Katie to become such a bully to her half-sister? He had hoped that the two of them would become good friends, but the opposite had become the reality.

CHAPTER 30

THE DARKNESS

He knew the first place to look for help was in Scripture and in prayer. He hoped God would show him the answers he needed to deal with all three of his girls. Without divine intervention, he knew he would fail. Somehow, he believed, God would lead him.

Thirty minutes later Dan emerged from his study, shaking his head in frustration. He had nothing. Why was God silent when he needed direction the most? His wife would be home before long, and he wanted to get things more settled between himself and Katie by then. And, there was supper to get started for the family, something his wife expected since he was always home first.

Upstairs, he found Katie in as foul a mood as he had ever witnessed. After knocking on her door, he slowly opened it and went inside. She sat on the edge of the bed, her arms folded to her stomach, her face streaked with tears; her defensive guard was up, aimed at keeping him at a distance.

"Katie," he began, softly. "You are my daughter, and I love you. And so is Cara. I just don't understand your treatment of her. What you said in the car...what's that all about?"

His daughter stood and moved away from him, refusing to face him or let him put his arm around her. "Mom knows. Just ask her."

"But I'm asking you. Talk to me."

136

Katie's stubbornness held firm. She refused to look at her father. He turned to leave but stopped to remind her that the discussion would continue later. Right now, she had house duties to fulfill. With that, he left the room in search of the other sister. "Who knows how far I'll get with her," he mumbled.

Eventually he found Cara in her private place, busy constructing her essay for the next day. It was something she had been writing in her mind since early morning, so putting it on paper was foremost on her agenda. She had put everything else on hold and was oblivious to her dad's sudden presence.

When he interrupted, she was writing the last line. He waited for her to finish before speaking. "Cara, I don't understand why your sister is so mean to you. That wasn't what I expected when I brought you here."

Cara, surprised at her father's statement, could think of nothing to say and just looked down.

The heavy silence made the space between them seem impenetrable and weighted him down even more. He fumbled with his thoughts and finally uttered softly, "You've really had a hard week, haven't you? How are you holding up?"

"I'm fine," was all she could think of saying. Her mind, however, was ablaze with all kinds of thoughts and questions, none of which she felt she could share. Finally, she ventured into the unspeakable, treading softly. "Why did you bring me here?" She couldn't believe she had said that.

There was a long silence, Dan trying to formulate an acceptable response. "First of all, I really am your dad. But I left your mom even before you were born. I've wondered about you for years, what you looked like, what kind of person you were becoming. When I knew your mom was dying, I decided it was up to me to finally be 'dad' to you. I thought it would be best. This way, you would be part of a family, my family."

Again the space around them was filled with a deep silence. The sound of Maggie's car in the driveway broke it, and Dan left, signaling for Cara to come with him. She left her essay on her writing box and tentatively followed.

Katie had set the table for supper, but when she heard the front door open, she rushed to get to her mom before anyone else.

"Mom, you won't believe what happened today. Dad got mad at me for saying Cara's not my sister. I told him you said so. Then he sent me to my room!" Katie's words came out fast and furious, a strong desire to get her story out first. She wasn't going to let anyone tell a different version.

"What happened? When was this?" Mom wasn't sure what she was hearing.

"In the car, on the way home. Something's going on in Cara's class about bullying, and I was trying to get her to talk about it in the car today. But Dad blew up!"

Dan and Cara arrived in time to hear most of Katie's lament. Once again he put his foot down, telling her for the second time to go to her room. Maggie was about to interrupt, but the look in Dan's eye told her not to. Cara made her way to where the boys were playing, hoping to avoid detection.

Meanwhile, Dan escorted Maggie into the office, closed the door, and tried to keep the conversation between the two of them. Dan's words were quiet and harsh; Mom's voice, too, was hushed, her words spoken through clenched teeth. Deep seated anger over unforgiven sins, building over the years, began to make their way to the surface in both of them; then, just as quickly, it stopped.

Maggie stormed out of the room. "I have children to feed," she taunted. And once again, the lid was put over the boiling pot. For the moment, things outwardly cooled to a simmer, but both parents knew that before long the situation would completely erupt.

The household spent the rest of the evening in fragile silence.

Even Jacob and Samuel felt the tension. In their innocence they had the audacity to verbalize their perception: "Is something wrong?" Jacob asked.

He was met with, "Eat your supper. It's almost time for bed."

"No bedtime story?" Samuel queried. His question was returned by a stern look from their mother. That was all it took. Everyone's bedtime was moved up, and as soon as the supper was cleared, Mom made her way upstairs. Katie followed, looking for the companionship she and her mom shared. Not tonight, she was told. Mom needed some space.

Cara, feeling the tension in the house, had tried to get to bed before Katie. That didn't happen, and Katie was waiting for her. "You're the cause of all these problems. You know that, don't you? Even your own classmates don't like you. You don't belong here."

"Why are you so mean to me? I never asked to come here. I'd go back home if I could. But I can't."

Neither said a word after that. Lying in bed, they both pretended to be asleep. It took some time before their raw nerves calmed enough for that to actually happen.

Dad took charge of getting the two little ones to bed. He even read them a story, hoping to help them fall asleep faster.

"Did you and mom have a fight?" Jacob innocently asked. "What makes you think that?" Dad asked.

"She never lets you put us to bed by yourself. She must be really angry."

Dan was amazed at the sensitivity of these little guys, as well as their innocence. "Let's just say we had some unkind words. Sometimes adults get mad, just like you guys. But we get over it. Everything will be fine."

With their clothes set out for the morning, Dan finished tucking them into bed. They said their prayers, and Dan kissed them both before wishing them a good night. Quietly he left the room.

Across the hall, the room where the two girls slept was dark, so he assumed the two girls were already asleep. What he didn't know was what had transpired a short while ago, while he was getting the two boys to bed. All Dan saw was that all the lights in the bedrooms were off, so he tiptoed downstairs to do some reading before going to bed. He was too wired right now anyway, feeling the tension of unfinished conversations, the weight of the problems heavy on his mind.

What had he done? Why had his plans failed? What was going on with Maggie that she still held his infidelity against him, even to the point of treating a young child this way? Was there anything that would change her, that would make her truly love him again?

It was quite a while before he decided to go upstairs and try to sleep. Even then it was fitful. His wife, too, on the other side of the bed, only played at being asleep while inside her heart was breaking all over again.

CHAPTER 31

FRIDAY

Friday morning breakfast was brief, everyone tired from a sleepless night. Cara retrieved her essay as everyone was exiting, and she was the last to climb into the van. No one spoke as she climbed into the back where she had the bench to herself. She was thankful for the separation between her and Katie and between her and the mother. Perhaps the distance would keep her safe. As it was, the ride seemed inextricably long on this particular day since no one was talking, not even the two little guys.

Eventually the silence was broken by the mother asking Katie if she was okay. "What's going on between you and your dad?" Katie just shrugged her shoulders. She was too tired and still too angry to talk about it. She had wanted her mom's attention last night. She wanted a time alone with her mom, not here with the big ears of her little brothers listening in, and not with Cara being privy to their conversation. So she said nothing, just looked out her window.

When they arrived at school, each person exited and walked separately to assigned destinations, the two boys slowly traipsing behind their mom. Everyone had their own distraction, it seemed. Anyway, it was Friday, and the welcome weekend was approaching.

While the events in the house were troubling, Cara's mind was on the paper she had written. Had she said what she meant to say? How would her classmates react? Was it okay? If Mrs. Clark approved it, Cara could read it to the class today. It was important to her, more important than anything else she had ever written.

She hurried to get to the room, hoping her teacher would be available. She was not. Cara felt disappointed, but she laid the essay in the middle of the teacher's desk where it would easily be found, believing that she could read it later on.

As it would happen, Mrs. Clark came in well after the bell, rushing to get the morning items taken care of and the class off to their regular Friday chapel. When Cara tried to speak to her about the paper, she was told to line up with the rest of the class; they were late – there was no time for a private conference; they would talk later.

However, 'later' never came. The whole morning seemed to be rushed, each class needing more time to get everything accomplished as it was. After lunch, the Spanish teacher arrived, and Cara decided the safest thing to do was to retrieve the paper from Mrs. Clark's desk. Instead, she received a reprimand for tampering with something on the teacher's desk, and her essay was put into the assignments box. Cara didn't take her eyes off it for the rest of the period.

When Spanish was finally over, Mrs. Clark returned for the last class of the day. Maybe, Cara thought, she could get her attention and find the essay. Once again it didn't happen. A speaker – a parent of one of the students – presented a science demonstration which took up the rest of the afternoon. Just that quickly, the class day ended.

Cara sat in her desk as her classmates exited the room for the weekend. What was she to do? Mrs. Clark owed her some time, and she was determined to show her the essay; it was due by Friday; that was the stipulation, and Cara would not let it go.

Finally, Mrs. Clark noticed her and remembered the incident from before chapel. "Oh, Cara! Your essay! I'm so sorry. This day just got away from me. Where is it? Do you have time for me to look it over, or do you have to rush out to the car line?"

Taking the essay out of the assignments' box, the two of them sat together, and Cara read her essay aloud. When she finished, there was a long silence in the room. Finally, the teacher spoke. "This was not what I was expecting." Cara's countenance fell. "Why did you choose to write this?"

"I just thought it would help." Cara's reply was soft. "When people are hurting, like Britney, Aubrie, and Caroline, the best help is to know how much God loves them. That's what I tried to say."

"You did more than that. This is beautiful. I'm so sorry we didn't have time for it today, like I had promised. Can we read it Monday?"

As they were talking, Cara's father showed up in the doorway, looking for his daughter; the others were waiting in the van, unless there was something wrong. Cara was asked to wait in the hallway; her teacher needed to speak with him for a few minutes.

Now what, Cara thought to herself. She thought about the week, about all the troubles in the classroom. Was that what the two of them were discussing? Was she in more trouble? That didn't make sense. Maybe it was about what was happening at home. No, her dad wouldn't talk with the teacher about that, would he? Besides, exactly what was happening at home? Even Cara wasn't sure of that.

When her dad finally joined her, they left. Thinking she saw her paper in his hand, she inquired about it. Yes, she was told, her teacher had given him her paper; and yes, he had read it. She wasn't in trouble, he reassured her. Just the opposite. He would talk about it with her later, when he would return it to her. For right now, he needed to keep it.

Cara tried to remember if she had written something she shouldn't have, something she had given away about her home life; was she in trouble or not? No, her dad had told her; and the teacher called it beautiful, also saying she would read it to the class Monday. Okay. But what was up?

Reaching the van, Cara saw that Katie and the boys had opened up all the doors in an effort to keep cool. They had been waiting at least 15 minutes, as Katie announced, and everyone was getting restless. "Where have you been?" Katie asked, accusingly. Then, more quietly, taking delight in chiding her half-sister, "In trouble, I suppose?"

The two boys, overhearing their older sister, picked up the comment and chanted, "Cara's in trouble! Cara's in trouble!"

"No, I'm not!" Cara's reply was louder than she expected, almost defensive.

Dad stopped the commotion, and the rest of the ride home was in silence. Once there, however, there would be matters that needed to be addressed. This can of worms was now open.

CHAPTER 32

THE ESSAY

It was Friday, and homework was put aside until Sunday night. Usually there wasn't any, so it was not a problem. Katie, who usually ran off to find her friend Maribelle, was told to stay close to home. So was Cara, who usually did anyway. Friday was usually a pizza night, and then the family liked to relax – maybe a movie on TV, book reading, even some kind of family activity, like a walk to the park and some playtime there.

Tonight, however, would be different. There was family business to settle when mom got home, and Dan had to decide the logistics of how to make things occur for the needed outcome. He decided to talk with Katie while he had the chance, before Maggie got home, before Katie would have the chance to defer to her mom. He called her into the office.

As soon as she walked in the door, the tension between them escalated. Dan caught her eye and quietly tried to reassure her, both of them knowing the seriousness of what they were facing. "We have some unfinished business," he stated, and Katie's angry look told him everything. He loved this daughter, but that was not what she understood, nor what her countenance returned; at the heart of the matter was what had transpired yesterday at this time.

Trying to reassure her of his love, she stood rigid, staring at him, her mental reserves taking over. In her mind, he had wronged her; he had wronged this household. He was not present in her earliest remembrances of "family". She remembered her mom crying; there was no dad in the picture. Then, when Katie was 4 years old, he showed up and moved them out of her grandparents' place, the only home she had known. They were starting over, she was told, and within a year, they had moved into this huge house. Their family grew to include two little boys, actual brothers she was told. Now, he had brought this 9-year old "daughter" from some other life, and she, Katie, was just supposed to accept her as a sister. She wouldn't! Her mom didn't want her, and neither did she!

Rather than waiting for her dad to speak further, Katie blasted away: "You can't make me like her! I don't want her in my room anymore! She's not my sister! Get her out of this house!"

Katie's words stung her dad. Instead of having the talk he intended, he spoke harshly, full of anger: "Katie, if you can't be civil, then go to your room. Now!" She ran out, crying, looking for her mom, her confidant, her defender.

While he was upset with himself, he knew there was nothing he could say to change the past; he needed his wife's intervention to deal with this, to put it to rest. She and Katie had a bond he couldn't break, no matter how much he tried. He had wronged them, and as much as he wanted the whole event to stay in the past, apparently it wouldn't. Now, with Cara's presence in their home, the evil was festering even more, and the infection was about to burst open. There would either be healing or further scaring. Whatever the outcome, it was time to face it.

It was only a short time before Maggie drove up to the house. Katie, who obviously was waiting at the bottom of the steps, ran to intercept her before she got in the door. As much as Dan wanted to speak with his wife in an adult conversation, he was way-laid by his daughter. Her eyes big and red, obviously from crying, she practically shouted, "Mom! You have to talk to dad! He's punishing me because of Cara!"

"What are you talking about? What happened?" Mom was obviously in her daughter's defense. "Dan, what's going on? What did Cara do?"

Dan's demeanor cued her in right away. He was dealing with something different. Somewhat smugly, she thought, maybe he was beginning to face what was going on right under his nose.

"Maggie, you and I need to talk. Katie, go back up to your room. We'll call you when it's time." Dad's manner of speaking was different somehow. Neither Maggie nor Katie argued with him, and Dan took his wife into the study with him, Cara's paper in his hand.

"So, exactly what did Cara do? You aren't honestly defending that illegitimate daughter of yours against a rightfully born child of *ours*, are you? Because if you are…"

"Margaret," Dan replied with a stern face. "Stop this!"

"Oh, *Margaret,* is it. What happened to *Maggie*? Or has she brought separation into this marriage again?"

"You're angry, and before you say anything else you'll regret, read this." He tried to hand Cara's essay to his wife.

"What? Did Cara write this, about how bad she has it here, how nobody loves her? Poor child! Better she had never been born…I've said that before, haven't I."

"Maggie," Dan implored more softly. "Just read it. Please, for my sake…for the sake of our family."

Maggie half-heartedly took the paper and in a mocking voice began to read aloud what Cara had written.

HURT AND FORGIVENESS

Sometimes life can be very hard. When that happens, it helps to know Jesus." (**Maggie's** voice began to soften.) "He always loves us, no matter what. When people say hurtful things to me, Jesus still loves me. I know, because that has happened a lot since my momma died. She's the one who taught me about forgiveness. (Maggie paused, staring at the paper, not sure if she wanted to continue. Finally, she did.)

Forgiveness is very important for us. We need to forgive each other every day. A lot of people think forgiveness means to say that what the other person did, their sin, is now okay. This is not true. If something is wrong, it's always wrong. Forgiveness doesn't change that. My momma said, 'Once a sin, always a sin'.

Some people think that forgiving and forgetting are the same thing. You forgive when you forget. This is wrong. We usually don't forget when someone hurts us. So that's not forgiveness either.

Some people say you just have to let it go. Over time, it will get better. No, it doesn't. In fact, sometimes it gets worse. Some people try to get revenge. They think the other person should pay for what they did that was wrong. That certainly is not forgiveness. We can never pay for the things we do wrong.

What I've learned is that forgiveness is all about Jesus. He already paid for all sins by his death on the cross. But, He has to live in your heart, and you have to give all the hurt to him. Don't hold on to it. Don't think about how bad you feel or how you're going to get back at someone. Just say, 'Jesus, this is all yours. I know you already suffered the pain of this sin, so just take this sin away also. Thank you. I love you, Jesus.' And then, every time the hurt starts to come back, you say, 'NO! I'm not doing that! I gave it to Jesus.' Sometimes it takes a while, but Jesus is stronger than anyone. Just hold on to Him because He's holding on to you.

With Jesus I will keep on forgiving people who try to hurt me. And I ask that He will stop their pain. Then they will be happy, too.

As Maggie read Cara's paper, her eyes began to fill with tears. Dan was the first to speak. "I'm sorry, Maggie, for all the pain I've caused you. I know I've said it before, but I don't think either one of us really forgave each other, really 'gave everything over to Jesus', as Cara said. We've tried to pretend that it was all over, all in our past, but by bringing Cara here, it's become evident neither of us let it go."

"Why did you bring her here, Dan? What did you think would happen?" Maggie spoke with a slight edge, showing the hurt she had held on to over the past 10 years.

"I'm not sure I thought of us. I only thought of Cara, how in losing her mother, she had no home, no family; it was time for me to own up to my responsibility toward her. I never thought what it would do to our family... to Katie, to you."

"Well, it's a little late for that now, don't you think? The damage is done. Again. Somehow I knew I would never be able to trust you. I just didn't think you would do this to our family." Maggie waved Cara's paper in Dan's face. "Who knows about us? Think about it! This paper is going to stir up questions..."

"Maggie, did you read her paper? I wonder if either of us ever really forgave each other." Maggie began to bristle when Dan said this. "Seriously, can you say that you haven't held my infidelity against me all these years? You just said it yourself...you knew you 'would never be able to trust me'."

Maggie said nothing, her attention turned to the paper; she sat silently, re-reading parts of what Cara had written.

Dan tried to continue the conversation with her. "Maggie, have you been honest about what happened to us? 10 years ago, I was wrong when I had the affair with Cara's mom, with Karina. But do you remember what was happening at home, between us? The infidelity wasn't just on my part."

"I never was unfaithful to you! I never took anyone into my bed!

That's what you did, not me!" Maggie's body trembled with her fury. She was about to storm out when Dan grabbed her arm.

"No, Maggie! That's exactly what you did! Oh, not physically, but in every other way. After Katie was born, you began to shut me out more and more. At first it was the afterbirth; then a safety matter – you didn't want to get pregnant right away; or, you were too tired to make time for us. I accepted all that. But then you went back to work, and still you had no time for me, for us. You shut me out! I was a new pastor at that time, overworked and overwhelmed, everyone expecting me to fill the shoes of their retired minister. 'He was a real shepherd,' they'd say…like I wasn't. I needed a wife. But you had taken another spouse – your own ambitions!"

Dan paused, and Maggie stood opposite him, her face turned to the wall. When he finally released his hold on her arm, she looked at him. "I guess finding an innocent young girl working in your office was pretty convenient, wasn't it?" Maggie spoke through clenched teeth. "What was your explanation? A 'poor, lonely girl, in need of a friend'? Oh, I remember; you said it just happened, only once. But she got pregnant? I never bought that story. Just how long did the affair go on? The truth, Dan?"

It took a few seconds before Dan was able to calm himself down enough to speak. "I never lied to you about that. Karina had just gone through the sudden death of a man who was about to ask her to be his wife. They were on their way to her parents' house for Thanksgiving dinner when their car was T-boned. He was going to propose to her at her parents' home; but instead, he was killed. She lived, but her injuries from the accident kept her from returning to college right away.

"She got a job helping in the church office - became a big helper for me; she knew everyone in the church, had grown up there. I came to depend on her. She was there when I needed help, when I needed someone to bounce things off of…and that was quite often. Our discussions grew more and more personal, but neither of us expected it to become intimate. We both regretted it right away. She even quit the job as soon as she discovered her condition.

"Later on, as people found out she was pregnant, it didn't take much to put two-and-two together; well, you know the rest. I lost my job, we had to move, I was removed from the clergy roster of the church and barred from the ministry, the only thing I had ever wanted to do in life!"

Maggie had listened skeptically. When Dan stopped talking, there was a pause before she verbally entered the fray. "Don't forget," she intoned. "You weren't the only one who lost a job! I had started the pre-school there. It was my baby. When we moved, I lost everything, including my self-respect. Moving in with my parents was embarrassing! Then you left to find work in a bigger city, and Katie and I were alone. Over the next four years of her life, she had an on-and-off father and two humiliated grandparents who had to explain their own daughter's failure.

"Then, suddenly, you came back with this grandiose plan to get back into the ministry. It was your calling you said. Forget about me, what I wanted, what I thought of it all. And we ended up here. Oh, yes, we've had more children. Two, to be exact. Was that your effort to show your commitment to me?"

At this, Maggie stormed out, leaving Dan to wrestle with what had again transpired. How could he get past his wife's anger? Where did they go from here? Had he messed up everything to the point where it could never be mended? In his office, he closed the door, very much wanting to be alone. What should he do now, he pondered. How could he deal with his wife's anger after all these years?

CHAPTER 33

THE RESOLUTION

Standing in the kitchen, Maggie began to sob. As much as she tried to hold it in, to be resilient, her eyes flooded and over-flowed with the anguish that had built over years of hurt and anger. Dan was right. She had never forgiven him because she had never acknowledged her part in their failed marriage. Throughout her life, she viewed herself and Katie as the victims. Little Cara had been an unwitting catalyst, and Maggie now realized Cara had been her scapegoat. How terribly she had been treating this innocent child. In her hand she still had Cara's paper. She read it silently, this time with a different interest, new eyes, as it were, eyes searching for healing, for a way out of this chaos that had taken over her life.

At that moment, Katie entered the kitchen, immediately picking up on her mother's distress. She saw Cara's paper in her mom's hands. "Mom, what's wrong? What did Cara do now?"

"Oh, Katie. I've been so wrong. I've wronged you, your dad, and now Cara. Where is she? I have to talk with her right now! Is she in the garage?"

"Most likely, in her hiding place."

"Her hiding place. Of course. Please go get her. Tell her to come here."

With a smug attitude, Katie went to the garage, to Cara's sanctuary. "Oh, Cara," she called in a mocking voice. "Mother wants to talk to you!"

Cara respectfully exited her refuge and solemnly walked inside.

"Cara," Maggie continued, "I've read the paper you wrote for your class. I…didn't realize…well, I…"

"Wow, Cara. What did you do now?" Katie taunted, a wicked glint in her eyes.

Maggie began to realize the enormity of the mistakes she had been making ever since Cara's arrival. She had both girls sit down with her at the kitchen table. Not knowing where to start, she picked up Cara's paper and began to read it aloud. "'Sometimes life can be very hard. When that happens it helps to know Jesus. He always loves us, no matter what. When people say hurtful things to me, Jesus still loves me. I know, because that has happened a lot since my momma died.'"

"Cara," Maggie continued, "I've treated you so terribly since you came to live here. I am so very sorry for the things I have said and done that have hurt you. I was wrong. I don't know if you can ever forgive me."

At this, Cara smiled ever so slightly, not being able to comprehend what was happening. "And Katie, I've wronged you, too. I haven't taught you about 'love and forgiveness'. I've been harboring such anger in my heart, there was no room for anything else."

Katie, feeling awkward, hesitated to respond. She had never seen her mother act this way. Now she began to feel guilty. What else had Cara said in that paper? Did she tell her mother all the nasty things she had said and done to Cara since she had come to live with them? Where was this going? Katie picked up the paper, and, sitting in a chair opposite her mother, began to read it to herself.

Cara cast down her face, not wanting anyone to see the tears welling in her eyes. She felt Maggie's hand gently caressing her shoulder. As much as Cara wanted to retain the hard exterior that had become her protection, something in her heart was melting, pushing away the fear. It was being replaced with a feeling that could almost be described as....*love!* Could it be? Were her prayers being answered?

As the three of them sat in silence, heads bowed in the solemnity of the moment, Dan came into the kitchen. Confused by the scene in front of him, he gently put his hand on his wife's shoulder, a silent prayer issuing from his heart. "Maggie," he finally spoke.

Standing, she wrapped her arms around him, sobbing heavily into his shoulder. "Oh, Dan. I'm so sorry. I never realized…I've been so wrong, so hurtful! What are we going to do? Can you ever forgive me?"

Dan's arms encircled his wife as he held her close. Caressing her, he reassured her of his love, asking her to forgive him, again, for all the hurt he had caused their family. "I know that with Jesus, we will get through this. And I think that's what's been missing in this house. *Forgiveness* was just a word we used to feel more guilt. Cara, what did you say in your paper? 'Forgiveness is all about Jesus', and about asking Him to stop the pain. Thank you, Cara." And with that, he picked her up and wrapped her in his arms. And now, Cara's defenses broke. Tears she had been holding since her mother's death flowed down her cheeks, her body sobbing heavily, her father enfolding her with such emotion and tenderness.

Katie wasn't sure how to act. She sat at the table, almost despondent, hoping her parents' former anger did not take a turn against her. But something was different. While her mother's arms were wrapped around Cara and her father, they looked at each other with such tenderness. She stood and walked over to the three of them, standing just slightly apart from them. She touched her mother, and when her mother looked down at her, she enfolded her in her arms, including her in the bundle of bodies. It seemed that at that point, another set of arms held them firmly, flooding them with His love. This was true forgiveness: Jesus taking their pain through His suffering and death on the cross, and giving them His love in return. This is what it felt like, this was the reality.

CHAPTER 34

LIVING WITH CHANGE

Over the next two days, things changed. Katie and Cara sat talking on the porch or in bed, Katie wanting to know what her mother was like, and especially asking what it was like to lose her. It gave Cara a chance to deal with some things she had not spoken of, to talk with someone closer to her own age about her feelings. Maggie and Dan made a point of tucking them into bed, saying prayers with both of them, kissing each on the forehead.

For Cara, things were different, but in reality, she still felt like an outsider. This was not her home, not her family. But what was? Dan and Maggie saw the evidence of the situation: Cara still maintained a protective circle, always being polite and helpful, but never letting down her guard to what was really happening to her on the inside.

Finally, they had a lengthy discussion that resulted in a long-overdue phone call. A decision was made on Cara's behalf: it was time for her to go home, back to where she had grown up.

Sunday night Dan brought her into his office. He looked at her thoughtfully before he spoke. "How do you feel about living here?"

"Oh, it's fine," she replied cautiously, not knowing what was coming.

"I'm not sure this is your *home*. Do you understand? Does that make sense?"

Cara looked at him with fear in her eyes. She wanted to tell him how hard she was trying to make this her home, to be part of this family. While things had gotten a lot better in just two days, there still was a certain awkwardness, and she missed her mother so very much. But where was her home, now? The only people she could think of were her grandparents, and she wasn't sure they wanted her.

"Where is my home?" she finally asked, trying desperately to hold back the fear that had begun to envelop her.

"Cara, you know your grandparents love you. They really helped raise you, along with your mother. And I think they miss you a lot! Wouldn't that be more home for you?"

With big eyes, Cara stared at her father. Something inside urged her to express her thoughts. Slowly, and with a hushed voice, she uttered, "But they blame me for my mother's death, don't you know that?"

"What are you talking about? Nobody blames you for your mother's death! Why would you think that?" He tried to bring her close to him, but she stood firmly, refusing his aid.

Cara had to compose herself enough to speak. At her father's urging, she finally confessed in a soft voice what had troubled her since her mother's passing. "I was supposed to take care of her; that's what my gramma told me. But my momma died! It was my fault! I didn't take care of her!" With that, Cara's steadfast resolve again broke, and sobs wracked her body with tumults that would not stop.

Dan marveled at this child's innocence. He had no idea what to say. "Jesus," he whispered in his heart, "give me the words." He had come to love this daughter. Knowing her would take much longer. He stood before her in silence, finally picking her up and gently enfolding her against his heart. "Cara, your grandparents do love you. And I'm sure they miss you. You're their only family now. Can you trust me on this?"

Although Cara outwardly shook her head yes, it would take a lot more to convince her.

CHAPTER 35

FORGIVING AND LEAVING

Monday morning, and Maggie personally escorted Cara to her classroom. She and Mrs. Clark were friends, but taking time to do this was unusual since she had a pre-school to run.

"Maggie? Good to see you! What's going on?"

"Good to see you, too!"

Both women smiled and gave the other a quick hug. Maggie continued, "I just wanted to make sure Cara has a chance to read her essay in class today. It's a life-changer!" Her sincere manner and her soft voice piqued Mrs. Clark's interest; she nodded her head in agreement.

Maggie continued: "There's one more important matter. Cara is going back to live with her grandparents. So, tomorrow will be her last day here."

"Oh! I'm so sorry to hear that! Cara, you're leaving us?" Mrs. Clark's manner showed her sincerity. Cara just nodded and went about getting her things organized.

There was small talk between the two women, and shortly Maggie left. Mrs. Clark approached Cara knowing the urgency that she be able to read her essay to the class. For Cara, it was an opportunity to express her understanding of how to deal with bullying. She had no animosity toward her abusers, but because she would be leaving soon, she wanted everyone to understand the necessity of forgiveness. Otherwise, she believed, things wouldn't change. Time had to be given in class for her to read the essay.

After a brief discussion, it was decided that she would read it at the beginning of religion class. Perhaps Cara would have a few comments of her own to add, if she was comfortable. She was, and she would.

There was another matter Mrs. Clark needed to discuss. "Cara, are you okay with leaving, with going back to live with your grandparents?"

Cara only nodded, still not convinced by her father that it would work out. Then, in her mind she heard her momma's voice saying, "One day at a time. Don't make tomorrow's troubles bigger than they are. Besides, Jesus is already taking care of them. You don't have to." Okay. She would try.

Her classmates soon flooded the room with their noise and busy-ness, and Cara was thankful for the diversions. Shortly, the bell rang signaling that school was to begin, and the class devotion was read by a student. Mrs. Clark then introduced their topic for religion class. She reminded them of the discussion they had on Thursday, the decisions made, and the items that would be signed and posted.

Next, she reminded them of the option to write an essay; and since Cara had done that, she would be allowed to read it now. Cara moved to the front. Standing tall, she read her paper, looking at her classmates on occasion, emphasizing each point. When finished, she actually began to play teacher, asking for discussion, questions, thoughts. "How will this help us with bullying?" she inquired.

The question played in the air awhile before one boy said, "Well, if you know you're going to be forgiven, what's the difference? Be a bully." A few people giggled. The student, however, was actually serious.

Other students began to berate him; he was wrong. That wasn't the point, they said.

"Well, what is?" Britney bellowed from the back.

Cara's fixed her eyes on her assailant; some classmates were ready to defend Cara, but they were unsure where this was going.

Finally, Cara spoke, picking her words carefully. "Britney, what you and Aubrie and Caroline did to me was wrong. You never should have written those nasty things. They really hurt me. But I forgive you. Do you know what that means? It means I'm giving you and your hurtful comments to Jesus. I'm not going to make them my problems. And, He already died and rose again to get rid of those things. So I have a victory over all your hate. What are you left with? That's up to you. You can keep bullying people, or you can let Jesus love you. What's your choice?"

Heavy silence filled the room. Try as they might, the three girls could not escape.

Mrs. Clark let it stand for several minutes before she intervened. "I believe Cara has given us something to think about. Let's put this on hold for now, let it mush around in our brains, and give it a chance to settle into our hearts." From there she ventured into a short discussion about the all-school Thanksgiving lunch the next day, and how that would change tomorrow's schedule.

As the period was coming to an end, she announced that Cara would be leaving, going back to her grandparents' home on Wednesday. Her classmates were shocked. Why, they wanted to know? Didn't she like it here? Some openly began to blame the classmates who had bullied her. That conversation was stopped abruptly. There were still two days before Thanksgiving vacation; make the best of it, they were told, and warnings were issued to be on guard – meaning, don't get into any trouble.

The rest of the day was noisy. Everyone, including the teachers, were ready for the break; no one was really interested in doing class work, so the teachers distributed seasonal puzzles and activities, had recess, and worked on whatever their part was in Tuesday's festivities. For Cara, this was strange: she finally felt like she belonged, and now she was leaving. Good thing God had it all in His hands, because it didn't seem fair.

Tuesday began with a special Thanksgiving chapel. The eighth graders presented their version of a "Christian Families' Thanksgiving", and a praise band of sorts added special music. Then, when morning classes convened, students from the seventh grade came in with a Thanksgiving game they had made up which included prizes. During the next hour, Cara and her classmates engaged in more of the puzzles and activities they had started the day before, including time for singing "Thanksgiving Carols". Just before noon, they made their way to the lunchroom for the special lunch, after which there was an extended recess.

The fourth grade class was called in early for a surprise: Cara's good-bye party. She received many homemade cards, all with the same sentiment: they didn't want her to go. Cara was dumbfounded. She had no idea they felt this way. Presents she received included drawing paper, crayons, colored pencils, candy, and a book to read – from Mrs. Clark, obviously. When the day ended, Cara needed a bag for all her stuff, which included the workbooks and papers from her desk. The bell rang, and a heavy sadness began to seep in, filling Cara with a sense of loss. Again!

Her dad came to her room to help gather everything. Cara had left a sweater there that Maggie wanted returned. Anything else? No, just a sad little girl with all her earthly possessions stuffed hastily into grocery bags. Mrs. Clark's good-bye hug was long. She didn't want to let Cara leave. But, it was for the best, or so she was told.

CHAPTER 36

THE HOMECOMMING

By nine o'clock Wednesday morning the van was packed, and Cara and her father were ready to leave for her grandparents' home. School was out for the Thanksgiving holiday, and the whole family gathered in the living room to say their good-byes. The two little boys clung to her fiercely, begging her not to go. Katie, too, was sad that Cara was going; she finally had gotten the sister she had wanted for so many years, and now she was leaving. All three were crying, their tears sincere displays of love for this sister who had spent so little time in their house. Even the mother gave Cara a hug and invited her to come back to visit, adding that this would still be a home for her.

At Dad's urging, he and Cara left. After all, it was almost a 3-hour drive each way, and he had to get back in time for the Thanksgiving service at church that evening. Cara sat quietly, looking out the front window; Dan was looking forward to talking with her, but she had once again reverted to the wall of protection she had acquired during her mother's final illness, shoring herself up to face the next chapter of her life.

Finally, he spoke. "Cara, is everything okay? You look like something is bothering you. Are you still worried about going back and living with your grandparents?"

"It'll be okay." Her voice was soft, unconvincing. She continued to look straight ahead.

"Yes, it will." He saw by the look on her face that she really didn't believe the words she spoke. "You know that Jesus is with you, and everything will be fine. Better than fine."

Yes, she thought to herself, Jesus is with me; and that's the only reason I'll survive whatever is coming.

Try as he might, Cara would not open up to him. He was unable to penetrate the outer façade Cara had established in an effort to protect herself, her system of protection having been well-defined over the years. Dan felt at a loss. While he understood her motives, he knew they were virtually unfounded – of that, he was sure!

Finally, he decided to just let it go – he really didn't know what else to say, and he firmly believed that Hank and Marion would have a better handle on what was happening than he did. After all, they had already raised one daughter, and they had known Cara since she was born. Instead, he spent the rest of the trip going over his sermon for the evening's service. That way, even if it was a little late when he got home, he'd be mentally prepared.

They finally arrived at her grandparent's house close to noon. Cara sat for a while before getting out of the vehicle. Then she saw her grandma, standing in the open doorway, tears running down her cheeks. Cara ran to her open arms; both of them held on to the other, heavy sobs wetting their faces. Suddenly, her grandfather was there, enfolding them both in his arms, his eyes slightly wet as well.

"You made good time," Hank said, looking at Dan. "Thought you'd have a lot more traffic."

"We got a good start, but the way home may be a bit longer." Dan smiled as the two of them shook hands.

Marion, her arms still full of her granddaughter, said, "Well, let's get your stuff in the house, Cara. Are you hungry? I have some lunch for you both. No sense you driving back with an empty stomach, Dan. Come on in."

Dan's big smile and gracious acceptance put everyone a little more at ease. There were things that needed to be said, Dan thought to himself, and a meal provided a comfortable setting that would make it easier. They visited, small talk as it were, over lunch: how his family was, what his schedule was like, were they putting in a garden this year, etc. Nothing noxious– just kind, simple talk.

After dessert, it was time for the serious things: he began with his apology for taking Cara. He realized, too late he said, that it was all about his needs and little to do with Cara. He continued by telling them of Cara's paper about forgiveness, the catalyst that changed things in their house. He also spoke of finally understanding Cara's need to be in this home, with her grandparents. With this he looked at Cara. She was staring at him, almost the same stare she had when he had first come to this house after the funeral.

"Cara," her gramma said, her voice somewhat hesitant, "what's wrong? Don't you want to be here with us?"

Cara said nothing, beginning to revert back to the behavior that had been her fortress over the past months, ever since her mother had gotten sicker and Cara knew she was dying.

"Cara," her father began, "you can tell your grandparents what you told me. It'll be okay. They love you."

The stillness of the room was heavily loaded with fear and uncertainty. Finally, a little voice said, "I'm sorry that my momma died." And then, Cara began to sob. It took a while for her to continue, but when she did, it seemed to pour out of her like lava from a volcano. "I know I was supposed to take care of her, and I really tried. But she died. I'm sorry! It was all my fault!"

Gramma wanted to hold Cara in her arms, but it was her grandpa who spoke. "Cara, none of us could keep your momma from dying. We all did what we could, you most of all I guess, but she needed healing from all her pain and sickness. That's what Jesus did; He healed her when He took her to live with Him. Do you understand? How could you think we would blame you? Oh, dear Cara."

And with that, new floodgates of tears opened; all four sat together in relief, knowing that here was the healing they all needed, here was the fortress – Jesus – that they trusted and relied on; here was the strength they needed to face all of life, right in the midst of them.

Dan left later than he expected. But his ride home was filled with the understanding that new life was about to begin, in both homes. Thanksgiving this year would have a more powerful meaning, all because of a new understanding of forgiveness, learned from a little girl who had been taught by a dying mother.

Printed in the United States
By Bookmasters